THE
COVENANTERS
OF THE GLENKENS

David S. Bartholomew

Published by
Carn Publishing Ltd.
Lochnoran House,
Auchinleck,
Ayrshire,
KA18 3JW.

© Rev Dr David S. Bartholomew, 2023

First Published in 2023

978 1 911043 21 8

Printed in Great Britain by
Imprint Digital Ltd.,
Upton Pyne, Exeter, Devon, EX5 5HY.

CONTENTS

ACKNOWLEDGMENTS

I owe the greatest debt to Dane Love, the Honorary Secretary of the Scottish Covenanter Memorials Association, for advice on the whole process of publishing a book, for doing the typesetting and for helping prepare the book for publication. I am grateful also to him for offering to publish the book under his label of Carn Publishing. Thanks are owed to my son Stuart and wife Heidi for assistance with the preparation of the maps for the book. The base maps for the two maps in the book were produced using openstreetmap.org, which has data available under the Open Database Licence. I thank the Scottish Covenanter Memorials Association for permission to use the photographs from their website of the gravestones of James Clement on Kirkconnel Moor and Robert Grierson in Balmaclellan churchyard; and John Sproat for permission to use his photo of me giving a talk in Balmaghie churchyard on the back of the book. Thanks also to Stephanie Haxton, Anna Campbell and Mike Brown for reading through portions of the text and making helpful suggestions for its improvement. I however take full responsibility for the final text of the book. The book expanded beyond the original plans I had for it and I could have continued happily following further fruitful avenues of research; but a time came when I had to call a halt and take the book forward to publication. The book before you is the end result of that process.

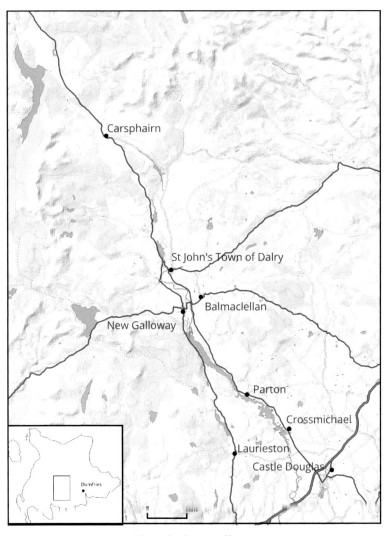

The Glenkens villages.
Base map: © OpenStreetMap contributors.

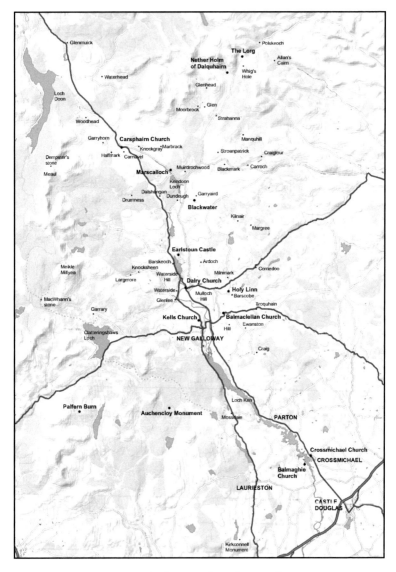

Location of places referred to in the text.
Base map: © OpenStreetMap contributors.

FOREWORD

When I was called to be minister of the Glenkens in 1994 I knew very little about the Covenanters. But I very quickly discovered that the four parishes of the Glenkens had been at the heart of support for the Covenanting cause in the 17th century and had suffered greatly when government sought to impose episcopalianism on the people. In this corner of the nation, far from the centres of power, the government effectively declared war on its own people. While many today in the parishes would struggle to articulate the reasons why the Covenanters took the stand they did, there still remains a deep emotional connection to the brave stand they took despite the injustices they suffered and the ruthless way in which the government sought to impose its authority upon them.

When I became aware of a number of local churches holding outdoor services (conventicles) to remember the faith and commitment of the Covenanters, I realised there were many inspiring, though often tragic, stories from the Glenkens that deserved to be better known. And so the practice developed of having an outdoor service each year to connect with the faith and commitment of our forebears.

When the Galloway Glens Landscape Partnership was looking for projects to enrich understanding of the history of the area for both local people and visitors the idea of a Glenkens Covenanter Trail seemed to fit well with that remit. It also seemed an appropriate opportunity to gather together the stories I had shared over the years to make them available to a wider audience. Prof Ted Cowan and I met with representatives of the Galloway Glens team a number of times to sketch out the plan for this trail. I enjoyed greatly the stimulus of Ted's great interest in this period of Scottish history and friendly banter with him and it was a great loss to the Glenkens and indeed to Scotland when he died; but I recognised from the outset that the onus was on me to do most of the groundwork for this project. Work commitments meant I couldn't give it the time it required and the years passed by.

Now that I am retired I am able to give more time to these matters and I believe my contribution to this project should be to provide a book that people will be able to use to explore the places around the Glenkens with strong connections to the stories of the Covenanters. The Glenkens has as its heart the four parishes of Dalry, Carsphairn, Balmaclellan and Kells, of which I was minister. But I have also covered to a lesser degree stories connected with the parishes of Balmaghie, Crossmichael and Parton, which lie to the south, surrounding the southern shores of Loch Ken. The stories require more space than a leaflet accompanying a Covenanter trail could ever supply. It is my hope though that in the future others might use this book as a resource to set out a Covenanter trail, perhaps with apps to enable those following the trail to engage with the stories. The Covenanter trail that was sketched out in our earlier discussions did not include some of the outlying places where I conducted conventicles; nor did it include some of the even more remote places connected with some of these stories. These are included in this book in order to enable the more adventurous to enter more deeply into the stories. I write this book to shine light on the rugged, independent spirit of the people of the Glenkens and of Galloway in those days, and to highlight the strong heart commitment they had to their Christian faith. The gospel had touched their hearts and brought inspiration to their lives, and they were willing to suffer persecution and even death rather than deny that faith and betray the Lord whom they loved.

I found Simpson's 1841 book *Traditions of the Covenanters* a great source of material on the Covenanters of the Glenkens. I am fully aware that I do not mention all the individuals to which he refers that deserve a place in this book. Simpson also shares the stories of John Ferguson of Wee Woodhead in Carsphairn parish and of John and Mary McClement and their daughter Janet who lived near New Galloway. There are others not mentioned by Simpson, such as James McGachen of Dalry, who was banished to the Carolinas in July 1684. We know nothing of his story – though he may well be the man that Wodrow in his book, *The History and Sufferings of the Church of Scotland*, refers to as James Magachen in Craigbuttock (Craigenputtock) in the Fugitives List of May 1684. But there are many other surnames on the fugitive rolls that are still found among the present-day inhabitants of the Glenkens. Each one would have had their own story of trials endured. And countless other unnamed individuals would have suffered the injustices of those traumatic years. In this book I try to open a window into their world to allow us over three hundred years later to experience something of what they endured.

1
THE HISTORICAL CONTEXT

The Glenkens has strong associations with the Covenanters. All the graveyards of the Glenkens contain gravestones and memorials to those committed men and women who chose death rather than compromising their beliefs and principles. But at a distance of nearly four hundred years it can be hard for us to understand the issues that drove them to take their stand.

At the time of the Reformation many people began to break away from the Church of Rome because of the corruption that they saw at the heart of the establishment. The details of that do not concern us here and over the years since then many wrongs in the Roman Catholic Church have been put right; but at the time it was seen as a very necessary step to reform the church. In Scotland, the Reformation precipitated a change in the way the church was governed. Each congregation came to have a leadership body called the kirk session consisting of a minister and elders, all of whom had equal voting rights when decisions were made. And, rather than having bishops ruling over a number of churches, the minister and an elder from each church represented their own church in a regional body called a Presbytery. Above this there was a higher tier called the Synod; and national decisions in the church were made at a General Assembly held annually attended by representative ministers and elders from all presbyteries. Thus Presbyterianism developed, under which church government was placed in the hands of leaders chosen from among those seen as spiritually qualified, both clergy and lay. In England however they decided to keep the Episcopalian system with bishops.

James VI (James I of England) did much to bring peace and harmony throughout the enlarged area over which he became king;

but there was one area where he found himself in conflict with the church in Scotland. As a monarch – and particularly as the godly one that he claimed to be – the hierarchical structure of episcopacy appealed much more to him. Without it he was concerned he would lose all control over the Church. As a result of his experience in England, he tried to push on Scotland the kind of doctrinal practices that were to prove so controversial during the reign of his son.

James VI was responsible for introducing bishops to the Church of Scotland when, in 1597, he managed to have an Act passed permitting bishops to be appointed and to be allowed to sit in parliament. The Church had agreed reluctantly to this, provided that such 'bishops' were elected annually by and were responsible to the General Assembly and they would not discharge any episcopal duties; they would in fact be 'commissioners', and not bishops at all. This compromise did not suit the king's plans, and in 1600 he used his royal powers, in defiance of the Church, to appoint four bishops to sit in parliament. When he became king of England as well, James determined to bring the Scottish Church into line with the Church of England and refused to allow the General Assembly to meet for several years. In 1606 he restored to bishops their episcopal rights and revenues, and in 1609 they were given judicial powers when the king created Courts of High Commission to try and punish anyone committing religious irregularities.

But while episcopacy was gaining a hold on the higher courts of the Church down at ground level various important events were quietly taking place – movements which were very soon to undermine the whole fabric of the religious hierarchy the Stuart kings were trying to establish. There was one thing that James VI and I had been scared to do, and that was to interfere with the lower courts of the Church. The kirk sessions, presbyteries and synods, composed of ministers and elders, still remained intact, and many of them were intent on holding on to their newly won democratic rights at all costs – even by defying bishops and king if necessary. The kirk sessions were well supported in many cases by the smaller land-owners who were the heritors of the parish churches, with responsibility for the upkeep of the church building and financial support of the minister. The parish was replacing the barony as the basic administrative unit; and the heritors and kirk session, working together, were taking over many of the functions of the old feudal barons. Parishes were becoming more and more self-contained units, responsible for looking after their own poor, and kirk sessions often dealt with civil as well as religious offences. In addition a school had to be established in every parish at the expense of the parishioners. All over south-west Scotland a new generation of common people, many of whom had now learned to read, was being raised. Their reading, however, was confined almost exclusively to the bible, and their spoken language, especially when passionately aroused, was biblical in style. And James had been behind the creation of a wonderful new translation of the bible into English which brought the Word of God in a fresh and inspirational way to his people. The folk of Galloway and Ayrshire especially soon came to identify themselves with the Israelite heroes of the Old Testament, and they regarded the Episcopalians as Philistines or other enemies of the chosen race.

After he left for England at the Union of the Crowns in 1603, despite his promise to return every three years, James only returned once to Scotland in 1617. By that time he had increased the number of bishoprics in Scotland to eleven and created two archbishoprics. In 1610 James reintroduced the administrative episcopacy by arranging for the bishops to be recognised as permanent presidents of presbyteries and synods, while at the same time arranging for much more generous financial provision for the church in the parishes. This compromise was accepted by many in Scotland, though less so in the south-west. When he arrived back in Scotland he was determined to press forward with his ideas for a uniform Church in his realm. He wanted to make various changes to practice and worship in the Kirk. He wanted Scots, like the

English, to receive Holy Communion kneeling; he wanted the Kirk to celebrate Christmas and Easter as religious festivals; he wanted new communicants to be confirmed by bishops, not by ministers; and he wanted private baptism and private communion to be permitted in cases of grave illness. Having produced his scheme for liturgical 'improvements', he left Edinburgh in August 1617 for the last time. The royal requirements he had issued became known as the 'Five Articles'. In November that year the General Assembly rejected them. The king was furious and the following year, despite much opposition, eventually a majority was mustered in favour of accepting them. King James banned any further meetings of the General Assembly. James engaged little with Scotland in the final, declining years of his reign and died in 1625.

His son Charles had none of his father's skill as a king and quickly alienated many of his subjects, both in Scotland and England. The nobility and a great many lesser lairds were terrified by the repeated threats of Charles I to resume possession of all the property in lands and teinds that the old church has possessed before the Reformation. Hardly a landowner in Scotland would have been unaffected if he had carried out his threat. The burgesses were feeling hardly less persecuted by the growing weight of taxation and municipal debt that Charles's financial policies laid upon them. Then in 1636 and 1637 the Crown published details of a new ecclesiastical policy which would have gone a long way towards assimilating the practices of the church in Scotland with those of the Church of England. It made no reference to General Assembly, Presbytery or Kirk Session, claimed that the king was the head of the church, obliged the Scots to accept a new prayer book with many echoes of previous Catholic practice, and also came close to forbidding extempore prayer. Only a man totally out of touch with the Scottish situation could have tried to push through such changes.

Things came to a head in St Giles Cathedral when an attempt was made to impose the English prayer book and the famous Jenny Geddes is alleged to have stood up and thrown her stool at the dean in protest. Shortly after this, churchmen in Scotland decided it was time to do something to protect their way of worship. They decided to band themselves together to resist the attempt to impose the episcopal system on Scotland. So it was they devised the National Covenant. A covenant is an agreement and those who signed it promised to adhere to and defend their presbyterian way of worship. In 1638 in Greyfriars Church in Edinburgh ministers, lairds, noblemen and commoners signed the Covenant; and soon it was being signed in kirks the length and breadth of Scotland. Those who signed it called themselves Covenanters, pledging themselves to keep the Covenant and to resist any attempt to impose episcopacy on Scotland.

The National Covenant was in three parts. The first part repeated the Confession of Faith of 1581, which renounced Catholic beliefs and practices and pledged to uphold Presbyterianism. The second part carried a long list of the various statutes and Acts of Parliament by which the Presbyterian Church had been established. The third part called for free parliaments and assemblies, and pledged its signatories to disregard Charles's recent innovations and to defend the Reformed religion 'against all sorts of persons whatsoever'. Despite its moderate tone and its appeal to the rule of law, the National Covenant was fundamentally a radical manifesto against the personal rule of Charles I and his arbitrary use of the royal prerogative. The Scots were looking to their national church for their sense of national identity, rather than to their king.

The king issued various royal proclamations against the Covenanters. Thinking that they formed a minority radical wing within the Church of Scotland, he agreed to allow a meeting of the General Assembly the first Assembly to be held since these meetings had been banned by his father twenty years earlier. It met in Glasgow on 21st November 1638, and sat for a whole month behind locked doors. It proceeded to depose the bishops and abolish episcopacy, and throw out the new Prayer Book. It was an open rebellion against the king and Charles resolved to raise an army and enforce his rule in his troublesome northern kingdom. (As an aside it should also be mentioned that this momentous Assembly also agreed to the creation of the new parish of Carsphairn, formed from the northern parts of Dalry and Kells parishes, and decreed that a collection be taken in all the churches south of the River Tay to endow this new parish church.)

By the spring of 1639 it was clear that war was inevitable. The Committee of Estates ordered the raising of levies in all parts of Scotland, and nowhere in the country was more responsive than Galloway. An enterprising Stewartry War Committee was set up with dictatorial powers to ensure that all the rules and regulations imposed by the covenant leaders in Edinburgh were enforced. Local regiments were set up and younger members of the nobility, landowners and staunch Presbyterians among the common people flocked to their standards.

Viscount Kenmure, who hailed from the Glenkens, was a leading member of the Stewartry War Committee. Another member was Alexander Gordon of Earlstoun, whose grandson Alexander we will meet later during the time of the persecution of the Covenanters. Alexander senior's great grandfather, Alexander Gordon of Airds in Parton parish, had been one of the pioneers of the Reformation in Scotland. On a visit to England he had met some of Wycliffe's followers and engaged one of them as a tutor to the family. He returned also with a treasured copy of the New Testament in English and in the years 1530-40 held secret gatherings in the woods near his house to allow others to hear God's word in a language they could understand. To hold such meetings was to risk his life. Alexander Gordon of Earlstoun had opposed the settlement of an Episcopalian minister in the parish of Dalry in 1635, for which he was fined by the Bishop of Galloway and banished to Montrose for a time. His son William was also a member of the Stewartry War Committee.

In the event the Scottish Covenanters' army proved too

strong for the king and his royalist supporters and little fighting actually occurred. In October 1640 a truce was signed at Ripon, and in the autumn of 1641 Charles visited Scotland where he addressed the Scottish parliament, agreeing to accept the radical constitutional changes he had previously opposed. He was to face the outbreak of civil war in England in 1642. When that war broke out the Scots were in a position of great strength, with a professional standing army. Both sides in England appealed to the Scots for help, and there was division in Scotland as to which side should be supported. The Covenanters won the day and it was agreed to support the parliamentarians. The Scots realised they were now in the driving seat and had a golden opportunity of exporting Presbyterianism and bringing English worship and ecclesiastical order into harmony with that of Scotland. In August 1643 they presented the parliamentary commissioners with the draft of a 'Solemn League and Covenant' which was as much a religious treaty as a military and civil pact. In exchange for Scottish intervention in the Civil War the English parliament would guarantee the preservation of the religious settlement in Scotland, reform religion in England and Ireland 'according to the Word of God and the example of the best reformed churches', get rid of popery and prelacy and confirm the 'firm peace and union' of Scotland and England. The English accepted the military part of the Solemn League, and in January 1644 a large Scottish army crossed the border. It was to play a crucial role in the parliamentary defeat of powerful Royalist forces in July of that year.

However the English were less enthusiastic about the religious aspect of the Solemn League. The Scots were allowed to participate in an assembly at Westminster which had been appointed by the English parliament to reform the English church. This assembly accepted an accord between their Churches (the Westminster Confession of Faith) and the English parliament eventually agreed to sign a modified form of the Solemn League and Covenant.

Some in Scotland doubted the English parliament's good faith. James Graham, the first Marquis of Montrose, was among them. He was a moderate Covenanter, but by instinct a Royalist. He switched sides and in February 1644 Charles appointed him to leadership of the Royalist forces in Scotland. He began his campaign by capturing Dumfries in March of that year; and just when his campaign seemed to be fizzling out he was joined by Highland and Irish forces. What followed was a remarkably successful campaign around the Highlands in the following year, defeating various Covenanter forces until all Scotland seemed to be under his control. However when marching towards England to join the Royalist forces there he was surprised by the Covenanting army returning from England at Philiphaugh near Selkirk in September 1645 and his army routed. Although Montrose escaped the field of battle he was a spent force and soon after left for exile on the continent.

Young William Gordon of Earlstoun had trained for the Church of Scotland, but when the Civil War broke out he joined the struggle and was given the command of a company in the Covenanter forces that were sent by the Parliament of Scotland under the command of General David Leslie to assist the English Parliament. When Newcastle was taken in October 1644 he was with one of his father's tenants' sons from Dalry who wouldn't allow his master to go first up a ladder in scaling the walls. They both reached the top of the wall at the same time, killed the cannoneer and turned the cannon on their adversaries in the town. They held out until others, admiring their bravery, flew to their assistance and they took the town. Soon after his older brother John, who would have inherited the estate, died aged only 30; and William was obliged to return home as his father was in poor health. He inherited the estate on his father's death in 1654, and never continued into full-time ministry.

The folk of Galloway were at the forefront in the decade beginning in 1645 in many of the political divisions which split the country. The first of these occurred as soon as Charles I was made prisoner in England in 1647, when some of the more moderate Covenanters tried to support the king and effect his release. But the plans of the 'Engagers', as they were called, were quickly foiled; first when their army was defeated by Cromwell's men at Preston; and finally when the Covenanters of Galloway and Ayrshire marched on Edinburgh with several thousand men to demand no more negotiating with the king. This was known as 'the Whiggamore Raid', and it was from these Whigs of the south-west that the great political party derived its name. The Whiggamores hoped to come to an understanding with Cromwell and welcomed him and his army in Edinburgh.

However the problem of the king's future was to prevent any accommodation between the two sides. The decision to try the king led to vigorous protests from the Scottish government. There was little doubt what the end result would be – the execution of the king; but the king of England was also the king of Scotland, and the Scots, while unhappy with his actions, still saw him as their divinely appointed king. Despite the Scottish protests the king was beheaded at the end of January 1649, and a few weeks later the monarchy was formally abolished and England became a republic. Within a week of the execution the Scottish Chancellor proclaimed the 18-year-old Prince of Wales, Charles, the new king of Great Britain, France and Ireland. However the Scots were resolved not to admit him to power until he gave assurances for the religion, unity and peace of the kingdoms.

William Gordon of Earlstoun was shocked when King Charles I was beheaded. Viscount Kenmure was also a supporter of the Royalist cause and suffered dearly for it when Kenmure Castle was captured and burned by some of Cromwell's forces in 1650. Initially William pinned his hopes on the late king's son, the future Charles II, accepting the Covenants. In 1653 he went to the Highlands with Viscount Kenmure to join the Earl of Glencairn in a Royalist revolt on behalf of the exiled king. He served with General Middleton when he came from France to command the

Royalist forces. But when the rebellion against Cromwell collapsed as a result of internal strife the following year, William and many others made their peace with Cromwell. William returned home, where he lived quietly and peacefully until after the Restoration in 1660.

In June 1650 the 19-year old Charles sailed from Amsterdam and landed at Garmouth on the Morayshire coast. He was accompanied by commissioners of the Kirk Party, which had come to power in Scotland after the defeat of the Engagers. It had its roots in the Whiggamores and relied on the corporate power of the ministers dictating government policy. The period from 1648 to 1650 has been called the 'Rule of Saints'. Pressure was applied to Charles to sign the Solemn League and Covenant and implement it in both Scotland and England. He resented this pressure but eventually bowed to their demands.

However England had just got rid of their king and had no wish for another. They were determined to resist any Scottish attempts to put Charles on the English throne. Within weeks Oliver Cromwell had been appointed Lord General and had crossed into Scotland with an army of 17,000 soldiers. He came face to face with a larger Scottish army of 22,000 at Edinburgh. Unfortunately the Scottish army had been purged of 'ungodly elements' and was far from the professional army it had been. The influence of religious zealots who arrogantly believed that God was on their side was strong, and this led to foolish mistakes and a devastating victory for Cromwell at the Battle of Dunbar in September 1650. Cromwell then entered Edinburgh.

At this point the Kirk split between the moderates, known as the 'Resolutioners', who were for king and Covenant and supportive of the Royalists; and the 'Protesters', the more extreme Presbyterians from the west and south-west who were for the Covenant and the Covenant alone. In the General Assembly of December 1650 the moderates won the day and the decision was made to proceed to crown Charles king, which duly happened on

New Year's Day 1651 at Scone. Charles began touring around the parts of Scotland not occupied by the English to gather support. Cromwell was keen to lure him south of the border where he was sure he could defeat him; and when Cromwell moved north to attack Perth Charles took the bait and headed south into England with an army, hoping to rally the population to his cause. However he found little support. Cromwell won a decisive victory over the Scottish forces at Worcester in September 1651 and Charles fled for his life, eventually managing to escape to France.

When Cromwell headed back south he left General Monk to continue to bring Scotland under the control of his forces, and by the end of 1651 the whole eastern half of Scotland, apart from Dunnottar Castle, was under English control. In December 1651 the English parliament passed a Bill incorporating Scotland into 'the free state and Commonwealth of England'. General Monk became Military Governor of Scotland and began building a series of forts around Scotland and establishing law and order. The only serious Royal revolt against the occupation was that referred to earlier under General Middleton which William Gordon of Earlstoun was a part of, but it came to nothing.

How did the church fare in the days that followed? During the days of the Commonwealth the authorities were unwilling to allow space for the Church of Scotland to exert any sort of spiritual authority. They wanted Scotland to be run by the middle classes rather than the aristocracy and the Kirk. They were happy for Kirk Sessions to meet, but forbade the General Assembly to do so. An attempt by the Protesters to hold an illegal General Assembly in St Giles Cathedral in July 1653 led to the ministers being evicted by soldiers and banished from Edinburgh or risk imprisonment. The minister of Carsphairn John Semple, was one of these ministers and he ended up spending six months in prison after having the temerity to interrupt Oliver Cromwell as he lectured the assembled gathering. But the ideals of the Covenant were not forgotten. They were merely driven underground until they came again to the surface in the tragic decades that followed.

After Cromwell died in September 1658 General Monk recognised that the days of the Commonwealth were numbered and that the return of the monarchy was inevitable. At the end of 1659 he began a march south with his army towards London, gathering support as he went. In London he summoned Parliament, which then recalled the king and afterwards dissolved itself. When King Charles landed at Dover on 25th May 1660 after sailing across from Holland Monk was waiting to greet him along with large, welcoming crowds. Present also was James Sharp, the minister of Crail and a moderate Resolutioner and Royalist. Monk had brought him south to act as a spokesman for the Kirk, and he was part of the delegation sent over to Holland to meet with Charles. He did all he could to calm the king's anger against Presbyterianism; but he failed in that venture and joined the opposition, and as Archbishop James Sharp he was later to pay for that with his life.

Charles II never returned to Scotland during the remainder of his life. After obtaining revenge over some of the Presbyterians who had humiliated him in earlier years, a new Scottish parliament was summoned to meet in January 1661. Every law that had passed since 1633 was annulled. It gave the king sole power to call and dissolve parliaments. The Covenants were declared illegal, and office-bearers had to swear an oath of allegiance to the new order. The Earl of Middleton, as Commissioner to the Scottish Parliament, was ordered to restore episcopacy – despite many advising the king to exercise caution on this matter. In June 1662 parliament passed an act which declared all parishes vacant whose ministers had been appointed since 1649, and that such ministers would have to seek the patronage of the local laird and confirmation from the bishop of the diocese in order to continue in post. The act was intended to remove the most prominent Protesters from their parishes. In the event over 300 ministers were deprived of their charges for non-conformity – nearly a third of the total number of ministers in the Church of Scotland. Many of them were in south-west Scotland, including all four ministers of the Glenkens, and the ministers of the neighbouring congregations of Parton, Crossmichael and Balmaghie; and the bulk of the members of these congregations left the churches along with their ministers. They stuck firmly to the Covenant and refused to accept the episcopal system. Nor were they willing to accept the king as head of the church, as they declared that this position belonged to Jesus Christ alone. Their allegiance was first and foremost to Jesus Christ and no other could supplant him. By law any person between the ages of sixteen and sixty who refused to attend the reintroduced Prayer Book services, at which roll-calls were taken, had to pay a heavy fine, the money to be collected by soldiers billeted locally. Rather than obey, confirmed Presbyterians escaped into the surrounding countryside, living rough, secretly nurtured by sympathisers, and holding open-air services or conventicles in quiet places in the hills, by burns, or up on the moors. Gabriel Semple, the minister of Kirkpatrick Durham, was given hospitality by Neilson, laird of Corsock, in Corsock House and conducted services in Corsock House until the numbers became too large, after which the meetings moved to the garden and then to the fields. These were the first conventicles to be held and were soon being replicated by Covenanters all over the country. William Gordon of Earlstoun was accused in 1663 of attending conventicles and admitted attending conventicles in Corsock wood and the wood of Airds, and also allowing deposed ministers to lead services in his house at Earlstoun and at his mother's house.

Harsh measures were taken against those seen as sympathising with the cause. The people of Dalry were fined more severely than any others in the Stewartry. Between 1663 and 1666 forty-three poor families in the parish were fined by the troops a total of £9577 Scots. In only three other parishes were fines of over £3000 collected – in Balmaclellan 49 families were fined a total of £6430, in Carsphairn 49 families were fined £4865, and in Irongray 42 families were fined £3363. Fines collected in Kells parish only amounted to £466, and in Balmaghie to £425 from 9 families; in Parton parish £2838 was collected from 24 families, and in Crossmichael £1666 was collected.

But these vast sums for the times still fail to describe the full extent of the misery inflicted on the people. If the offender could not pay their fine at once, their goods were seized and sold or they had troops quartered on them to eat them out of house and home. Women and children were molested and made to suffer all manner of indignities at the hands of the soldiers. The more defiant had their homes burned down and hundreds were made homeless, having to resort to living in the woods or in turf and stone shelters they built on the moors. Galloway was effectively under military occupation and relatively out of sight, away from the seat of power, the troops abused their position to take advantage of the local populace. The cruelty of the troops and the injustice the people suffered simply served to drive the majority of the population in the Glenkens to sympathy for the Covenanting cause. For many young lads, accustomed to the monotonous and heart-breaking task of wresting a living from the infertile fields of impoverished crofts, the life of a Covenanter became an adventure full of romance and excitement, and they felt they had justice on their side. On the whole, the Covenanters sought to offer peaceful resistance and to avoid as far as possible the shedding of blood. But almost inevitably in the face of such severe persecution there were some who became so incensed at the injustices meted out that they responded more forcefully.

Things came to a head in the Pentland Rising in 1666, which could more accurately be called the Glenkens Rising for it started in Dalry. Four Covenanters who had been hiding in the hills, including McLellan of Barscobe, came down to Dalry to seek a brief respite from the harsh November weather. They found an old man being tortured by dragoons and came to his rescue, injuring one of the soldiers. It began a popular uprising to protest against the injustices being perpetrated in Galloway. Many Covenanters rallied to join those who had begun marching on Dumfries and when they reached that town they were able to capture Sir James Turner, who was in charge of the local military force. They then made their way back through Dalry and up to Ayr and then on to Lanark, gathering others along the way. After passing through Bathgate they came round by Edinburgh and were attacked by superior government forces at Rullion Green in the Pentland Hills. Some 50 were killed and another 80 taken prisoner, including 30 women and children. More died as they fled for their lives, and the survivors were hunted down throughout the land. Five of the prisoners sent to be tried at the court in Ayr were from the Glenkens and were among the seven who were executed on 27th December 1666 and buried in a martyrs' grave in the Auld Kirk graveyard there – John Graham, John Short and James Smith from Dalry; and James McMillan from Muirdrochwood in Carsphairn parish and Alexander McMillan from Carsphairn parish. John McCall from Carsphairn parish was executed up at Irvine and John Neilson, the Laird of Corsock, was executed in Edinburgh. There was to have been an eighth hanged at Ayr. However after the Ayr hangman ran away and the Irvine hangman refused to conduct the executions, the authorities offered freedom to one of the condemned men if he hung his companions. Cornelius Anderson, a tailor from Ayr, was the only one who volunteered – but only after he heard from the others that they forgave him for what he was about to do. He was required to perform the executions at Irvine also, and was never able to recover from the guilt and trauma of what he had agreed to do.

After the ruthless response to those who took part in the Pentland Rising, there came a time known as 'The Accommodation' when a more conciliatory approach was tried by government. In January 1668 an Act was introduced which required all nobles, heritors and tenants to take a bond on behalf of themselves and their servants to keep the public peace. Acceptance of this oath resulted in a free pardon, even if they were known to have sympathies for the covenanting cause. The only exceptions were some 60 of those seen as extremist Covenanter leaders who were still to remain outlawed. The majority of Covenanters in Galloway however were suspicious of this approach from government, fearing they would be called to compromise in how they lived out their Christian faith. In May a long list was compiled of those Galloway land-owners and tenants who refused the bond. The list for Carsphairn parish has 21 names on it and the lists for Dalry, Kells and Balmaclellan parishes 17, 8 and 6 names respectively, showing that the Glenkens was still staunchly anti-government. However, although a proclamation was issued for their arrest, the persecution that followed was not as harsh as it had been in the previous years.

On the list of those seen as extremist Covenanter leaders not given the opportunity of a pardon we find the name of Robert Cannon younger of Mondrogat (Muirdrochwood) in Carsphairn parish. He had been an active leader of the Pentland Rising. When the Covenanter force moved on from Lanark towards Bathgate Mondrogat was left behind briefly with some men to destroy the ferry-boat and hold up Dalziel's advance. He was injured at the Battle of Rullion Green and, bleeding badly from a wound, urged Sir James Turner to flee with him, hoping that he might use him as a bargaining tool if any of the rebel officers were captured, and threatening to shoot him if he refused to come. But Turner resisted and urged him to flee to save his own life, which he did.

For a long time he eluded capture, but in a letter to the Privy Council at the end of September 1668 Charles II mentioned that he had heard that Mondrogat had recently been captured and desired that a special effort be made to extract as much information from him as possible. The king clearly saw Mondrogat as a key figure amongst the Covenanters. For a long time Mondrogat held out and refused to divulge any of the information that was sought. In the end however the pressure on him from the authorities became so intense that it broke him, and in early August 1669 we read that he had submitted information helpful to them and most likely come to an agreement with them to provide information to them in the coming days, and in the light of that there was a petition from him expressing his sorrow for his accession to the late rebellion and asking for the king's mercy in granting him his freedom. The king granted his request and at the beginning of September the Privy Council ordered the city magistrates to set him free if he signed a bond to keep the public peace.

Mondrogat was zealous in serving his new masters. In the following years he became notorious for leading the soldiers to some of the Covenanters' favoured hiding places. He was made the exciseman, or tax collector, for Carsphairn and the neighbourhood and, as he knew everyone, the soldiers used him to identify those they apprehended. He became a powerful figure, greatly disliked and feared in the district.

On 30th September 1669 there was an attack on John Row, the curate of Balmaclellan, which is described in detail in the Privy Council records. He was already in his night clothes when, at nine o'clock at night, three armed men came to his home. The men, one of them dressed in women's clothes, broke down his door and entered the house. None of them spoke a word and one of them, with dirk in one hand and a baton in the other, violently assaulted the curate and beat him to the ground, treading on him with his feet, and beating and bruising his naked body; until the other two, who were guarding the door with drawn swords and pistols, urged him to stop. Then, while the man in women's clothes guarded the door, the other two went through the rooms of the house with lighted candles gathering up his bed clothes and other clothes and his furniture and breaking open his chests and rifling through his books, papers and money, including the poor box of the parish. What they could not carry away they damaged and destroyed. Then, just after they had left, the man who had previously assaulted him came back in and again beat him to the ground and, dragging him along the floor, declared that he was a dog of a man who had come in upon honest men's labours. Then, threatening him, he made Row swear that he would live no longer in that house or preach in that church; after which he continued to beat him senseless before leaving to re-join his companions.

Some local people, including the outed minister, Thomas Vernor, and his father-in-law James Grier of Milnmark, were called before the Council and charged that, even if they hadn't committed the actual offences, they were guilty of aiding and abetting the perpetrators and should be charged under the law for this; also declaring that the heritors and parishioners of Balmaclellan parish should be required to make restitution for the damage caused. However it was acknowledged later that they and the parishioners of Balmaclellan had no involvement in the attack. One of those responsible was John Smith of Dalry, and at the beginning of December the Privy Council records mention that he had been arrested and placed in the prison in Thornhill, from which he had escaped. It is likely that he was later caught, as one of the Covenanters who survived the 1679 shipwreck in the Orkney Islands while en route to slavery in the Carolinas was a John Smith of Dalry. This man was most likely recaptured and suffered banishment on a later vessel.

In April 1671 John Row gave a commission to John Maxwell in Threvegrange to uplift from the heritors and others in Balmaclellan parish all the stipend requirements owed to him for the years 1668 to 1671. Clearly he had done little to endear himself to his parishioners; but, despite the threats he had suffered, he continued in the post of minister of Balmaclellan until 1672, when he moved to Stoneykirk in Wigtownshire. He was the son of the Principal of King's College, Aberdeen. In 1686 he renounced the Protestant faith and converted to Roman Catholicism.

But meantime there had been a further attack on a local curate a little outside the Glenkens. On 3rd November 1669 three men in disguise came to the house of John Lyon, the curate of Urr, at eight o'clock at night. The curate himself was not at home, but they saw through the window his wife lying in bed. She had given birth to a child only 36 hours earlier. Holding up a pistol, they threatened to kill her if she would not open the front door. She called the servant woman to open the door for them; and then while one guarded the door the other two dragged her out of bed clad only in her nightshirt and pulled her through the house, looking for her husband. When they couldn't find him they held a pistol to the servant woman demanding to know where her master was and the location of his best possessions. They then proceeded to gather his books, clothes and everything else of value and carried them all off. John Lyon declared that his parishioners were not responsible for the attack and asked that some other means might be found to reimburse him for his loss. It is likely that this attack was carried out by the same three individuals who had attacked the curate of Balmaclellan,

A report to the Privy Council on the same day (2nd December) revealed that John McCallum of Brockloch had been arrested and had admitted to having taken part in the Pentland Rising and also to have assisted in some way those responsible for the attack on John Lyon. The Privy Council declared that he should be held responsible before the Justices for these crimes. The case next came up on 3rd March 1670 when a petition from John Callan (McCallum) of Brockloch and William McEwan in Langtoun was considered. They declared from the tolbooth of Edinburgh that they had been held prisoner since the previous November and pleaded that they might be released and all the writs, papers and bonds confiscated from them returned to them. The Lords gave permission to the Edinburgh magistrates to release them provided that they promised to sign the Declaration agreeing to live in a peaceable manner in the future and that they paid John Lyon £600 Scots for damages. They called for John Callan to pay £30 sterling and William McCuin £20 sterling. Furthermore they granted full power to the petitioners to pursue and apprehend the persons guilty of the robbery and gave them the right to reclaim from the robbers the money paid to John Lyon.

In 1669, in response to a letter sent to London from both

outed Presbyterian ministers and members of the privy council appealing for reconciliation, Lauderdale was sent north as a Commissioner to the Scottish Parliament and later that year he issued his 'First Indulgence', which allowed 42 dissident ministers to return to their parishes in return for a bond promising good behaviour – to live peaceably and exercise their functions in the established church, but not requiring them to denounce the Covenants. Those Presbyterian ministers who were prepared to have their appointments confirmed by the local bishop were then to be paid their full stipend. But significantly, ministers who still refused to acknowledge the Episcopalian system were also allowed to return to their charges and have the use of the manse and glebe; however they did not receive a stipend, but had to rely on their congregations to provide for their needs. One condition of the Act of Indulgence however was that conventicles should cease to be held and that all who attended such meetings should be dealt with severely. A new Act was also passed in 1672 calling for annual celebration on 29th May of the Restoration of the king, and for ministers to preach on that day and give thanks to God for this. A 'Second Indulgence' was issued in September 1672, which allowed another ninety ministers to return to parish ministry. But at the same time field preaching was made a capital offence.

The more extreme Covenanters were unwilling to accept these restrictions on their freedom to worship and were often suspicious of the indulged ministers, whom they felt had betrayed the cause. And indeed some of the indulged ministers, avoiding topics of a controversial or political nature, lacked the fire and charisma of those ministers who refused any compromise with the authorities. Despite the ban on conventicles such gatherings continued to be popular and opposition to the government more defiant. Many outlawed individuals dwelt in the hills, supported by sympathisers and fearful of their hiding places being betrayed to the authorities by others without sympathy for their cause.

The arrival of the 'Highland Host' under Graham of

Claverhouse in the west and south-west in 1678 ushered in the final decade of persecution of the Covenanters. The Privy Council unleashed 6000 highlanders on this troublesome part of the realm to teach it a lesson. They plundered and pillaged and returned home with much booty stolen from the inhabitants during the four months at the beginning of the year. Ayrshire and Wigtownshire suffered most, but there are records of their forays into Carsphairn parish and they may well have ventured further south into the Glenkens.

With the authorities determined to stamp out conventicles and dragoons likely to shoot on sight if they came across such gatherings, many Covenanters were now armed for protection. Things came to a head soon after the murder of Archbishop Sharp at Magus Muir near St Andrews in a chance encounter with some Covenanters in early May 1679; this resulted in a new determination on the part of the authorities to deal harshly with all who supported the Covenanting cause. When Claverhouse and his troops attacked a conventicle at Drumclog in Ayrshire on 1st June 1679 the Covenanters put up stiff resistance and the government forces were put to flight. However later that month Claverhouse was part of a government army under the Duke of Monmouth that won a decisive victory over a Covenanter force at Bothwell Bridge in Lanarkshire on 22nd June.

It is interesting that there is in the Kirkcudbright Sheriff Court Deeds the record of an attack on the house of Alexander McGhie of Balmaghie, the 9th Lord of Balmaghie, on 11th June by some Covenanters from the Glenkens. William Gordon of Dundeugh, William Gordon of Craig, Robert Gordon of Garrary and his brother James Gordon in Largmore, and George Roan younger in Stroanpatrick, along with servants and accomplices attacked McGhie's house, stealing 'plate, swords, money, guns, pistols, eddles, bridles' and other items for which they were each fined £5 Scots for riot on 26th August. It is likely that they were seeking to equip themselves for the coming conflict.

The Covenanters had been emboldened by their success at Drumclog; but splits in their ranks between those who were moderates and desired to seek justice and an end to the oppression suffered, and those of a more extremist position who were unwilling for any compromise, led to chaos in their ranks and inevitable defeat. An ill-armed Covenanter force of about 4000 foot-soldiers and 2000 men on horseback was faced by a well-organised government force of 15,000. By the end some 400 Covenanters had been killed and 1400 taken prisoner, while only a handful of government soldiers lost their lives. William Gordon of Earlstoun arrived late when men were already fleeing from the scene of the battle and was shot dead by a party of dragoons. His two servants, John Ramsay and John Tilly, gave themselves up and later were able to return to Dalry. William's son Alexander managed to escape and return back to the Glenkens.

Most of those taken prisoner were kept for over four months in open cages in the churchyard of Greyfriars Kirk in Edinburgh – the notorious Covenanters' Prison. Kept in crowded conditions in the open air and given very little food, a number died. The numbers however steadily dropped as time went by as many of the more moderate Presbyterians were willing to accept the king's peace and take the oath never to rise in arms again and obtain a bond for their good behaviour; they were then released. In the end the remaining 257 prisoners were herded into the hold of the *Crown of London* to be banished into slavery in the American Plantations in Virginia. Tragically the boat was shipwrecked at Deerness in Orkney on 10th December and only some fifty of the prisoners survived. Many of these men were recaptured and shortly after shipped to slavery in Jamaica and New Jersey. We know that John Malcolm and John Smith from Dalry survived the shipwreck, as did John Edgar from Balmaclellan and Robert Caldow from Balmaghie. James Houston from Balmaghie perished and probably David McCubbin from Dalry. There is uncertainty as to whether David McCubbin came from Dalry or from Dailly in Ayrshire.

The divisions among the Covenanters widened even further after Bothwell Bridge. After the battle Richard Cameron, the spiritual leader of the 'Cameronians', returned from Holland. The Cameronians were those Covenanters of a more extremist position. Cameron gathered around him a band of those who were unwilling to reach any compromise with the government and were inspired by his radical preaching. On the 22nd June 1680 the anniversary of the Battle of Bothwell Bridge, Cameron and a band of his supporters entered Sanquhar and nailed to the Mercat Cross a defiant Declaration, declaring themselves representatives of the true Presbyterian Church and covenanted nation of Scotland. In the Declaration they rejected the kingship of Charles and, asserting they were under the standard of their Lord Jesus Christ, the Captain of Salvation, effectively declared war on the king and all those who stood with him. Amongst that group were James and Daniel McMichael, Robert Stewart and John Malcolm, all from Dalry parish. Cameron had hoped that his stand would lead to a popular uprising, but a month later, on 22nd July, a detachment of 120 dragoons caught up with Cameron and sixty of his men at Ayrsmoss, just west of Muirkirk. The dragoons suffered more casualties than the Covenanters, with the loss of 28 men, but Richard Cameron and his brother were killed along with seven further members of his band. Most of the Covenanters got away, but five survivors were rounded up and taken up to Edinburgh where they were executed. The following year the Test Act was passed to tighten control over the nation.

The passing of the Test Act in 1681 led on to increased persecution in Galloway. People at all levels of society were required to acknowledge the king's authority in all matters, ecclesiastical as well as civil, and to renounce the Presbyterian form of religion. Not surprisingly people with strong religious convictions were unwilling to swear the required oath, whether they were covenanter extremists or not. The authorities were often heavy-handed in the way they managed the situation, holding courts in a parish on a certain day which all the inhabitants between the ages of 16 and 70 years were required to attend to take the Test. Often the curate was in attendance to vouch for the faithfulness of the person in attending church or otherwise, and individuals would be questioned on whether they had attended any conventicles. This imposition only served to increase opposition to the government and stiffen resistance to such oppressive policies. More people took to the hills to avoid taking the Test and were hounded by the troops stationed in the area.

In May 1684 the privy council drew up a Roll of Fugitives for Galloway and on this appear the names of 209 men and 12 women who were outlawed and sought after. Some 82 of these people belonged to the four parishes of the Glenkens. People were ordered not to comfort or harbour these fugitives and do all in their power to apprehend them. It should be noted that this roll makes no mention of wives or younger members of families, who were often fugitives as well.

By the autumn of 1684 the government had greatly strengthened their garrisons in the troubled areas and issued them with new orders for the persecution of relatives of the outlawed Covenanters. The privy council passed an Act which empowered the military to kill Covenanters anywhere and at any time. It was partly in response to the Apologetic Declaration of James Renwick, a native of Moniaive who had taken over the leadership of the most extreme covenanters after the death of the Cameron brothers at Ayrsmoss. The Apologetic Declaration hurled defiance and abuse at the king and his ministers and threatened immediate death to all informers. It was secretly fixed to kirk doors and market crosses all around the south-west. The government retaliated immediately by introducing the Abjuration Oath which people all over the south-west were required to take in addition to the Test, thus renouncing completely the terms of Renwick's Declaration. The new Act declared, 'The Lords of his majesty's privy council do hereby ordain any person who owns, or will not disown, the late treasonable document (the Apologetic Declaration), whether they have arms or not, to be immediately put to death.'

Robertson, in his book, *The Story of Galloway*, writes as follows (p.167):
'It was the Act which opened the period, covering the autumn of 1684 and the whole of 1685, that came to be known in the history of the Covenanters as 'the Killing Times'. Courts were now virtually unnecessary, for anyone could be shot on the spot, or even more cruelly done to death, without any need for trial or proof of guilt. Examination of the records of those killed in this way reveals the following facts:- Some of the victims were undoubtedly fanatical Covenanters, rebels, and therefore guilty according to the law; some more clearly quite harmless creatures whose only crime was that their consciences would not allow them to swear away their presbyterian beliefs by taking the Test or the Oath; others were quite obviously completely innocent.

Records have been compiled giving details of the deaths of 82 persons who were summarily killed by the troops in Galloway during 1684-85. Once again, of course, these numbers are by no means complete, since they represent only those whose deaths were witnessed and recorded. All over the more desolate parts the covenanters were being massacred by the soldiers and their bodies left to rot on the heather where they fell. No records were kept of such killings; the victims were simply regarded as 'missing', for none of their relatives or friends knew how or where they had died. For many years after the Killing Times shepherds were continually finding on hills and moors the bleached skeletons of Covenanters who had been killed in this way.'

King Charles II died of a stroke on 12th February 1685. The Killing Times continued until May of that year, but after that the time of oppression eased. Charles's brother James had governed Scotland faithfully as his viceroy from 1680-82, but when he became king he was treated with suspicion on account of his conversion to Catholicism. Within a few months he faced armed insurrection in both Scotland and England, though that came to nothing. James was determined to put behind him the years of conflict and promote religious tolerance. His 1687 Declaration of Indulgence was designed in particular to help Roman Catholics but extended to Protestant non-conformists as well. It granted unlimited toleration to all religious denominations. All were allowed to 'meet or serve God in their own way, be it in private houses, chapels or places purposely hired or built for that use'. Conventicles however were still banned. This Act dismayed Episcopalians, who saw it as the thin end of the Popery wedge, but it was welcomed by the Presbyterian Church. Preachers and activists began to come back from exile in Holland. Conventicles were still held, but there was not the political resolve to make an issue of this. Indeed some of the more extreme Presbyterians took the step of opening new meeting houses, independent of the 'official' church.

James reissued the Declaration of Indulgence in April 1688 and ordered all the bishops of the Church of England to distribute it and have it read from every pulpit on two consecutive Sundays. This order was ignored by most clergymen and seven bishops, including the Archbishop of Canterbury, denounced it and were thrown into the Tower for sedition. Then in June the queen give birth to a son, giving the promise of a continuing Catholic line. This was more than the country could tolerate. In the Netherlands William of Orange, whose wife Mary was James's daughter from his first marriage and had been next in line to the throne before the birth of the baby prince, had been growing increasingly concerned about the prospect of a Catholic England. He let it be known that he was willing to come over and help ensure the nation remained Protestant. At the end of June 1688 a group of seven Protestant nobles invited William of Orange to come over with an army. He duly did so at the beginning of November. At that point James lost his nerve, recognising that support for his reign was draining away, and at the end of December escaped to France. In January Parliament recognised that the throne had become vacant and declared James's daughter Mary Queen and that she should rule with her husband, who would be King. In April the Parliament of Scotland declared James to have forfeited the throne of Scotland as well.

With the assistance of French troops James came over to Ireland in March 1689. The Irish Parliament supported him and declared that he remained King. James worked to build an army in Ireland, but was ultimately defeated at the Battle of the Boyne on 1st July 1690 by an army under the command of his son-in-law, William. He fled to France again, never to return to his former realms. In England William's claiming of the throne became known as the 'Glorious Revolution' because it had been achieved without bloodshed. In Scotland that was far from the case. John Graham of Claverhouse, now ennobled to Viscount Dundee, had gone south to support James in 1688, but had arrived too late to be of any assistance to the king. He returned to Scotland and initiated the first Jacobite Rising. On 27th July 1689 there was a great loss of life when the two armies clashed at the Battle of Killiecrankie. Many lives were lost on both sides and Dundee himself was killed, but the clansmen gained the victory. 'Bluidy Clavers', the ruthless persecutor of the Covenanters, was to become better remembered in the years that followed as 'Bonnie Dundee'.

After Killiecrankie the much depleted government army retreated to Perth. The government in Edinburgh ordered the Cameronian Regiment with 800 men under Colonel William Clelland to head for Dunkeld. Clelland was only twenty-eight years old, but a seasoned soldier who ten years earlier had had command of the Covenanter army that defeated Claverhouse at the Battle of Drumclog. When they arrived at Dunkeld on 17th August 1689 they began building defences. On 21st August a Jacobite army of four thousand men appeared and stormed the town. The two sides fought fiercely from house to house all day, until the Cameronians were on the point of defeat. However at that time the exhausted Highlanders decided to retreat. Both sides had lost many men and

Clelland himself had been killed. The threat from the north to the security of the kingdom had been laid to rest, at least for the time being.

In June 1690 the Scottish parliament passed an Act restoring Presbyterian government and discipline in the Church. The Church was given the right to purge its ranks of any ministers deemed to fall short of what was required, an action that became known as the 'rabbling of the curates'. This allowed many former parish ministers to return to their charges. The times of trial and persecution had come to an end.

2
THE SOURCE OF THE STORIES

I have found Robert Simpson's book *Traditions of the Covenanters*, which was published in 1841, a very helpful source of stories from those troubled times. Simpson writes in the typical flowery language of the time and certainly rather romanticises the whole story of the Covenanters. But I have come to the conclusion that he has preserved a remarkably accurate record of things that happened in those days. I believe he tapped into the folk memory of the local people and gathered up stories that had passed down the generations by word of mouth. So inevitably there are some inaccuracies. But he has managed to capture a vivid snapshot of life in those troubled times. An example of information that he received by word of mouth is preserved in his account of Roger Gordon of Largmore: '(Roger) then repaired, with all convenient speed, to his accustomed hiding-place in one of the lofty ranges of the Galloway mountains, called the *Mill* or *Meaul ae*.' This was Simpson's attempt to write down the name of this mountain, which a few years later was rendered as Meikle Millyea by the Ordnance Survey in the first edition of their map.

At first I could find no historical record of some of the individuals Simpson mentions in his stories, which for a time concerned me. For instance, the names of neither McRory nor John Fraser are found in what seems a comprehensive list of those called 'disorderly' for not attending church in Carsphairn parish. I have yet to find any outside proof of the existence of McRory. However in the Kirkcudbright Sheriff Court Deeds of 1694 there is mention of a tack given to 'James Clark, younger, now dwelling in the Nether Holem of Dellquherne of the fourth part of the two and half merkland of the said Nether Holem, as presently possessed by James McMichell, James Clerke, John Frizell and herself (Janet Corsane), with the pertinents and teinds thereof, lying within the parish of Carsphairne' (see under 'McTurk' on the Carsphairn Heritage Archive website).'Frizell' is the anglicised form of the Gaelic Friseal, the gaelicised form of the surname Fraser.

I then discovered that there is a John Frizzel mentioned in the 1684 Fugitives' List under Dumfriesshire – 'the son of Thomas Frizzel in Auchincairn'. Auchencairn is a farm two miles southeast of Closeburn. We find numerous mentions of the Frizell/ Fraser family in the Privy Council records in the latter half of 1684 after the Enterkin attack when some Covenanter prisoners were set free. There were numerous sightings of John Fraser recorded around Auchencairn and also Glenmead, where Andrew Fraser (his brother?) is said to be living. There is also mention of Margaret Frizell in Mitchellslacks, the mother of William and Thomas Harkness. The Harkness family were involved in the Enterkin attack and it is probable that Margaret was Thomas's sister and the Harknesses were therefore part of the extended family. In the end Luke, Thomas, Andrew and Sarah Fraser spent several months in the Canongate Tolbooth in Edinburgh for assisting rebels. I found a further mention of John Fraser in the Privy Council records of August 1684, where James McTurk in the Holm of Dalquhairn in Carsphairn parish was accused of conversing with John Fraser and John Clerk in Marbrack, rebels. So there is plenty of evidence for the existence of John Fraser. I thought perhaps he moved to Carsphairn parish as a young man if, as Simpson maintains, in earlier days he attended Carsphairn Church alongside Robert Cannon of Muirdrochwood, who later turned informer.

However I then came upon a further piece of information which suggests perhaps Simpson embellished his story of John Fraser with details that he could not substantiate. If this further piece of information is correct it would imply that Fraser and his family only moved to the Upper Holm of Dalquhairn at some point during the times of persecution. John Crichton, who published the *Memoirs of John Blackadder* in 1826, includes in his book a long footnote in which he draws on a paper in his possession which recounts the persecution suffered by the people around Kirkmahoe during Covenanting times. He writes, 'One John Frissel in Auchencairn had offered some refreshment to six men who were pursued, and had fled for safety to his house, about twelve o'clock at night. A party of dragoons came upon them, and seized one of the fugitives, John Glover of Barshel, and carried him to prison, being severely wounded and abused, where in a short time he died. The soldiers returned and spoiled Frissel of all he had; they pulled down his house, dragged himself, wife and two daughters to prison; one of his daughters they banished to New Jersey.' Perhaps when he was released John Fraser decided he should look for a fresh start with his family in a place where they would be less troubled by the dragoons. In a financial contract he entered into with James Roan, merchant in Stroanpatrick, in January 1674, he is recorded as living at Holm of Dalquhairn; so he had clearly moved to the Glenkens by that date. He was still living at the Holm of Dalquhairn in February 1694, but by November 1695 had moved to Woodhead in Carsphairn parish.

Simpson is the only one who records the story of John Dempster of Garryaird in Dalry parish. However in the Register of the Privy Council of Scotland, we find reference in October 1667 to Dempster of Carridow (Corriedoo, on the boundary between Balmaclellan and Dalry parishes) who was one of the principal characters proscribed after the Pentland Rising; and in May 1668 mention is made of William Dempster in Hill in Balmaclellan parish who was also involved in the Rising. So it is clear that members of the Dempster family were living in the vicinity and supportive of the Covenanter cause. Furthermore I came across a 1669 bond of caution taken out in Edinburgh by John Dempster in Greenhill for John Gordon and others in New Galloway, that the latter would not molest John Reid, provost of New Galloway, and others in New Galloway, along with their families, tenants and servants. I am not sure of the location of Greenhill, but clearly this John Dempster had an active presence in the area. I also came across a 1664 contract of marriage between Margaret Dempster, daughter of Simon Dempster, and James Milligan in Clauchrie. Clauchrie was just to the east of Corriedoo. The contract was signed at the Mill of Glenlee, mentions Simon's youngest son William and was witnessed by Alexander Gordon in Kilnair, which is not far from Corriedoo – all pointing to the Dempster family residing in the Corriedoo area.

Further research in the Kirkcudbright Sheriff Court Deeds built up a fuller picture of the Dempster family. I suspect father Simon was the 'Dempster of Corriedoo' singled out in October 1667. The deeds record him as living at Corriedoo in October 1666. In January 1660, along with his son Andrew, he obtained an 11 year tack from Roger Gordon of Troquhain to Slangaber and Westland at the northern extremity of Kirkpatrick Durham parish and deeds on both 8th September and 3rd November 1666 record him as living at Westland, which I see as evidence that he spent time at both places. After that we lose sight of him, suggesting that after Pentland he was lying low to avoid capture. Given the lack of further mention of his name it is likely he died soon after Pentland. From the deeds we find out that Simon had sons Andrew, Robert, John and William, and also daughter Margaret, who married James Milligan in Clauchrie, and a further daughter who married Edward Neilson in Knockwalloch. Andrew is recorded as living at Corriedoo in 1655, but from October 1691 onwards is recorded as living at Margree, just to the north. There are records of Robert living at Blairinie, just north of Troquhain, from May 1671 to March 1675. William is recorded as living at The Hill, Balmaclellan from May 1666 to April 1673. In December 1675 he is recorded as living at Ewanston and in May 1689 as living at Margree, while the Fugitives' Roll of May 1684 mentions a William Dempster in Ironmacannie in Balmaclellan parish, so he seems to have moved around a bit more. There is also the record of a James Dempster in Tower in

Dalry parish in 1658 and 1660 who may have been another son. However John is noticeably absent from the record, apart from the time he witnessed a deed alongside his brother Robert in January 1663 and the record of the bond of caution he took out in 1669 up in Edinburgh. Perhaps John Dempster had been working as a tailor in the vicinity of New Galloway but to avoid capture after the Battle of Bothwell Bridge sought refuge in the more isolated Garryaird, where he is said to have resided at the time of his death.

THE GLENKENS MINISTERS

It is interesting to consider what happened to the four parish ministers of the Glenkens after they were put out of their churches in 1662. Thomas Vernor, the minister of Balmaclellan, took on the tenancy of a small farm on the shore of Lochinvar in Dalry parish, close to Milnmark, where his father-in-law James Grier lived. He was granted indulgence to return to his parish in 1672; he did not observe the anniversary of the Restoration of the king in 1673; but there is no record of him losing half his stipend, so perhaps he was no longer receiving one. In 1679 he was accused of preaching at conventicles, and in February the following year his parishioners were prevented from paying him any stipend. He was declared fugitive in May 1684. He is recorded to have ministered at a number of field conventicles and to have baptised a number of children at them. He returned to his pulpit after the troubles and died in 1716 as the longest serving minister in the whole of the Church of Scotland. William McMillan of Caldow in Balmaclellan parish had been licensed to preach by the ministers in Northern Ireland around 1673, where he had gone to escape persecution and spent much time in prison for preaching at services in private houses and attending field conventicles. Cross-examined before the Privy Council in Kirkcudbright in October 1684 he mentioned that Thomas Vernor's wife had recently attended a service in his own house, so clearly she was committed also to the Covenanting cause.

John Semple of Carsphairn had a strong influence on

the Covenanting cause in Galloway. Even before he was formally deprived of his charge he had spent six months in jail in Edinburgh in 1653 for standing up to Oliver Cromwell; he was also arrested at a meeting of members of the Protesters Party at a private house in Edinburgh in 1660 just after the Restoration of Charles II and spent ten months in prison in Edinburgh Castle. When he was released he was deprived of his charge and it is unclear whether he returned to Carsphairn. We do know that at the end of December 1666 he claimed to have been living quietly in Currie just outside Edinburgh the previous fifteen months. However in September 1672 he was granted indulgence to return to his parish as minister. He was fined in 1673 for not celebrating the Restoration of the king and lost half his stipend, a penalty which John Cant of Kells and John McMichan of Dalry also suffered. In 1677 he ran into more trouble with the authorities, but died soon after in his own bed.

John Cant of Kells was deprived of his charge in October 1662, but he appealed against this decision and in March the followed year he was allowed to continue in his charge. He later confessed to having broken several of the instructions given to indulged ministers. In 1684 Peter Peirson, the curate of Carsphairn, in a report to the Privy Council accused Cant in three instances of baptising the children of Carsphairn parish. Peirson declared that as an indulged minister Cant only had the right to preach at Kells, and not to baptise the children of another parish. He was brought before the Justiciary in December 1684 and then appeared before the Council the next month and his bond taken that he would live peaceably and not preach. He was restored in 1689 under the Act recalling Presbyterian ministers but stood down as minister of Kells in May 1689 on account of poor health.

John McMichan of Dalry was deprived of his charge in October 1662, after briefly being imprisoned in Edinburgh in June of that year. In July 1669 he became the indulged minister of the parish and was able to return as minister, though the following year he was fined for failing to observe the Restoration and lost half his stipend. He was brought before the Justiciary in December 1684 and then appeared before the Council the next month and his bond taken that he would live peaceably and not preach. His wife was a first cousin of William Gordon of Earlstoun and he was able to purchase the estate of Barcaple in Tongland parish in 1687. He was restored to his charge in 1689 and died a few years later.

Fig. 1: 'Burning Bush' Covenanter Sculpture, Dalry.

3
ST JOHN'S TOWN OF DALRY

In 2004 a new sculpture commemorating the Covenanters was dedicated in Dalry (Fig. 1). Bill Dunigan, a member of the Scottish Covenanter Memorials Association and Managing Director of Mayfield Engineering Ltd in Sheffield, had offered to donate a steel sculpture to the Association in memory of the Covenanters. It was decided that this should be erected in St John's Town of Dalry to mark the starting point of the Pentland Rising, one of the most significant events during that time of conflict. This was considered to be a particularly appropriate location for it, given the lack of any memorial recording this momentous uprising and given the central role that Dalry played in the whole Covenanting struggle. The sculpture, which is five metres high and weighs three tonnes, represents the burning bush that Moses encountered in the wilderness (Exodus Chapter 3). The lower part representing the flames was fabricated from corten steel, which weathers naturally to a reddish rust colour; and the bright shining leaves, formed of stainless steel, represent the lives of the saints who are never burnt up or consumed despite going through times of trial and persecution and even suffering death. On some of the leaves are inscribed the names of well-known Covenanters, most of whom died for their faithful stand. The sculpture stands alongside the playpark beside the main road between Ayr and Castle Douglas.

THE PENTLAND RISING
On 13th November 1666 Robert McLellan, the laird of Barscobe in Balmaclellan parish, an ardent Covenanter, came down to Dalry with three companions. They had sought refuge in the hills from the predations of Sir James Turner and his dragoons, but the cold

and the rain and the need to replenish their supplies forced them to come down briefly from their upland shelter. On the way down they passed three or four soldiers who were stationed in Dalry driving before them some poor men that they had ordered to thresh the corn confiscated off an old man by the name of Grier, who had fled to the hills rather than paying fines for non-attendance at church. Though filled with indignation they kept quiet, for they were relieved that the soldiers were occupied with other business and did not stop them, and they needed to seek food and shelter. They were welcomed into an ale-house at the top of the village which stood where the house in Midtown 'The Cush' now is and there were grateful of the warmth and hospitality. They were still finishing their breakfast when some upset villagers rushed in to say that the soldiers had returned, dragging Grier with them, whom they had caught in his own house. They had bound the prisoner and were threatening to strip him naked and place him on a hot grid-iron as a punishment for not paying his fines, and no doubt also to extract from him information on the whereabouts of other Covenanters.

Barscobe and his friends left their breakfast and hurried to the rescue, demanding of the soldiers why they had bound him. "How dare you challenge us!" was the reply. A scuffle ensued during which the soldiers drew their swords. At this point one of Barscobe's companions drew and fired a pistol laden with small pieces of clay tobacco pipe and wounded one of the soldiers, and the others surrendered. The wounded soldier was Corporal George Deanes. He was carried on horseback to Dumfries where he arrived at six o'clock the next evening. He later petitioned the Privy Council on the ground that he was "barbarouslie shot in the bodie with a great many pieces of tobacco pipes, ten whereof afterward were by the surgeon's care taken out".

Barscobe and his companions realised that after injuring a soldier their lives were forfeit, and they resolved to seize the moment and try and raise a rebellion against the injustices they were being forced to suffer. They called others to stand with them and then they headed for the village of Balmaclellan. Some of the faithful had gathered near there for a conventicle, and strengthened by some of their number, they surprised the soldiers stationed in Balmaclellan and took 16 prisoners. Recognising that Sir James Turner, when he heard what had happened, would exact a terrible revenge, they decided to seize the initiative and head for Dumfries, where he was based. The call went out through the country – by the bush telegraph of the day – that all who supported the Covenant should meet at Irongray Kirk just outside Dumfries on the following night (14th November), with the intention that they might enter Dumfries at daybreak.

At Dumfries Turner was in no position to cope with even a minor revolt. In October his cavalry had been withdrawn. He had barely 70 men at his disposal, all of whom, apart from 12 or 13 at Dumfries, were policing the surrounding district. Barscobe and his friends had already reduced his force by nearly a third. Nor was his health very good at the time. News of what had happened at Dalry and Balmaclellan reached him on the evening of the 14th when Corporal Deanes was carried in full of "tobacco stopple", and he sent out an instant summons to his men in the neighbourhood to come into Dumfries by 9 o'clock the next morning to gather ammunition and then march on Dalry.

Meanwhile, many supporters of the Covenant began converging stealthily on Irongray along tracks away from the main roads. By daybreak about 50 horsemen and two hundred men on foot had gathered. About nine in the morning they approached the bridge into the town, which was unguarded. Leaving the infantry at the bridge end, the fifty horsemen under the command of Barscobe rode into town. A small party of four, Robert Neilson of Corsock among them, hurried forward to Turner's lodgings.

Turner had risen about six, but when almost dressed had begun to feel unwell and decided to go back to bed again for a time. The clatter of horsemen in the street below roused him. Clothed only in his nightgown he appeared at the window and demanded the business of those below. They responded that they required his surrender. Turner's version of what happened next differs somewhat from that recounted by the Covenanters, and I suspect there was an element of trying to paint a better picture of himself in his memoirs compared to the truth of what actually happened. We are fortunate to have in his memoirs [*Memoirs of His Own Life and Times*, available online], a detailed account of the whole journey up to Rullion Green in the Pentland Hills near Edinburgh. The Covenanter version has him in a blind panic appealing for mercy, saying there will be no resistance. And Neilson, described as a meek and generous gentleman (and even Turner admits that) replies: "If you come down to us, and make no resistance, on the words of a gentleman you shall have quarters" – in other words, your life will be spared.

On the strength of Corsock's assurance, and despite his servants' protestations, Turner descended and surrendered clad only in his night-gown, night-cap, drawers and socks. The welcome that greeted him down below was not quite as generous as he'd hoped. In the meantime the self-appointed commander of the Covenanter force, Captain Andrew Gray, had arrived and taking out his pistol would have shot Turner in his scanty and incongruous attire had not Corsock protested, "You shall as soon kill me, for I have given him quarters." Turner's personal effects were not treated so kindly. His room was ransacked, and Andrew Gray took possession of a coffer filled with his papers and money.

The sudden raid on Dumfries had amply repaid the daring and rashness of such an exploit, and the band was suddenly faced with the challenge of what to do next. Gray and his party decided it was wise to demonstrate that their seizure of one of the Government's officials was not to be construed as an act of political revolt. With Turner in their midst, scantily clad in his night-gear and mounted bare-backed on a little beast with a halter on its head, the captors proceeded to the Town Cross where, to show their loyalty, they drank the king's health. [Turner comments that the beast he was given was Captain Gray's own animal, for the good reason that Gray had helped himself to a far better horse of Turner's!] From the Town Cross they passed through the town and out through the Nether-port to reach the banks of the Nith opposite the kirk of Troqueer. Turner was apprehensive, given that there was clearly lively debate about what should be done with him. However compassion won the day. Recognising that their captive was hardly clad for a winter journey, they returned to his lodging in Dumfries where he was allowed to dress himself more appropriately. It could be added that the weather that November was particularly inclement, and one chronicler of events remarked that from the day of the insurrection in Dalry right up to the clash at Rullion Green there was not a fair day, but only stormy days of wind and rain. We might pity the bedraggled party making their way through the countryside on foot along muddy tracks.

With Turner more fully clothed, and weapons seized and distributed among the infantry, they set off in the afternoon for the kirk of Glencairn near Moniaive. They got there in the evening and Turner was allowed to enjoy hospitality at the manse there. But they were anxious to press on and headed on during the night for Dalry – according to Turner more than half now mounted on horses with swords, pistols and carabines, the rest on foot with muskets, pikes, swords, scythes and forks. Turner was their only prisoner, apart from his drummer who was determined to stick by him, as a little before Gray had released the rest of the captured soldiers and told them to cause no further trouble. Turner's condition forced them to ride but slowly, and they stopped briefly at Castlefairn where the woman of the house showed compassionate concern for Turner's poor health. They continued on and Turner remarked that one of his guards, Canon of Barnshalloch in Balmaclellan parish, entertained him the whole night with warnings that he was about to die and he should prepare for it and repent of all his heinous sins, especially of his persecution of God's people, those who faithfully kept the Covenant.

The next morning they came to Dalry, where their number increased to 250. There the Rev Hugh Henderson, who had lately been the popular minister of Dumfries but had been deprived of his position in 1662, asked permission of Captain Gray that he might have Turner dine with him at his house just outside Dalry. In passing it should be mentioned that Henderson was probably a Glenkens man and had returned to his Dalry roots after he had been evicted from his church in Dumfries. He had been appointed to serve as minister of Carsphairn in 1638 before it became a new parish and after that was minister of Dalry until 1643. The General Assembly had then sent him to Ulster for five years, after which he had gone to be minister in Dumfries. Turner comments that although they were of different persuasions, Henderson entertained him with real kindness and encouraged the Captain to set him free.

That night Turner lodged with Captain Gray across the river at Waterside, the home of Mr Chalmers, who entertained him with much courtesy and civility. However he wasn't able to rest for long because a report arrived that a body of horsemen had been spied nearby on the River Ken and Gray forced Turner to get ready to ride north, speaking abusively to him about his slowness in responding. It proved a false alarm and he was allowed to go back into the house. But Captain Gray was decidedly on edge and at 11 or 12 o'clock that night he decided they would carry on anyway. Turner writes, 'Very dark it was, it rained pitifully, the wind was loud, and the way exceedingly bad; yet sick as I was, I was forced to ride eight miles to Carsphairn, where the Captain lodged me in a country house, with 15 horsemen to guard me. I spent the rest of the night till day in that poor house, as well as I could.'

Gray was still his companion, but early next morning he suddenly disappeared. The day before he had sent off to a safe destination the money and baggage he had seized at Dumfries. A lot of mystery surrounds the question of who exactly Captain Andrew Gray was. It would seem he was unknown to the rest of the band of Covenanters, but had come with an order that they should obey his authority and come under his command. The general conclusion was that he was a man who took advantage of the confusion of the times and decided to slip away with his loot while the going was good. They never saw him again.

Gray's sudden departure added further confusion to an enterprise that was still without settled plans. Barscobe, Corsock and a minister by the name of Robinson assumed command, and they spent the day where they were. They sought a better house and in the evening Turner was sent to the house of Gordon of Knockgray. The man himself was in prison in Kirkcudbright, but his son entertained Turner very well for some favours done to his father. However he also had to entertain 30 horsemen who were sent to guard Turner.

The next day the host headed towards Dalmellington and then on through Ayrshire towards Edinburgh where finally, despite brave resistance, they were routed by superior government forces on 28th November at the Battle of Rullion Green in the Pentland Hills. You can read an account of the whole journey to Edinburgh in *Memoirs of His Own Life and Times* by Sir James Turner himself, which can be accessed online. Traditionally this march on Edinburgh has been known as the Pentland Rising. But it might more accurately be called the Glenkens Rising, for it was an incident in Dalry that sparked the uprising against the injustices of the time. It should also be emphasised that there was no desire on the part of the Covenanters to seek armed conflict with the government forces. They took weapons for self-protection, but at heart there was a naïve belief that if they brought the injustices they had been suffering to the attention of the authorities in Edinburgh it would bring them relief from their unfair treatment. As mentioned earlier, a Covenanter sculpture was dedicated near the southern entrance to Dalry on 18th September 2004 in memory of those troubled days.

ROBERT MCLELLAN OF BARSCOBE

Robert McLellan of Barscobe became deeply involved with the Covenanting movement after the incident in Dalry recorded above. His castle lies just to the south of the Holy Linn in Balmaclellan parish (Fig. 34). He led the band that headed towards Dumfries after the injury of the government soldier, and the horsemen that crossed the bridge into Dumfries and rode up to Sir James Turner's residence were under his command. The Covenanter force that was routed by government forces at the Battle of Rullion Green in the Pentland Hills a couple of weeks later was by then under the command of James Wallace, an Ayrshire man who had served in the Parliamentary army with the rank of lieutenant-colonel in the English Civil War; but under his leadership were Major Joseph Learmont and Robert McLellan of Barscobe. At Rullion Green Wallace stationed Barscobe and his Galloway troop of 80 horsemen on the right, and on the left the main body of horse under Major Learmont. The superior government forces won a decisive victory in the engagement that followed, in which Robert's brother Thomas was killed. Though injured, Barscobe made it back home to Galloway. In the following months the authorities actively sought after all those who had been involved in the rebellion. In October 1667 an Act of Indemnity offered a reprieve to all those who had taken part who were willing to take a bond to keep the public peace; but that offer did not extend to those, like Barscobe, who were seen as particularly responsible for the uprising.

In April 1668 a number of people, including Sir William Bannatyne, claimed they had recently seen Barscobe walking around openly in Edinburgh. Then in June 1670, at what was to become known as one of the first 'armed conventicles' at Hill of Beath near Dunfermline in Fife, at which John Blackadder preached, Barscobe was there with 9 or 10 of his Galloway men. When a local militiaman arrived Barscobe saw him as a threat and moved to challenge him, at which point Blackadder stopped the service and came over to defuse the situation and ensure there was no bloodshed. Barscobe was also at the Battle of Bothwell Bridge in 1679 with a troop of horse, and in October 1681 he was named in a proclamation against those being pursued after Bothwell, alongside his brother Samuel. His estate was to be forfeited because of his continued rebellion against the government.

On 9th March 1682 there was an appeal for mercy before the Privy Council from his 18 year old nephew Thomas Neilson, who was being held in the Canongate tolbooth. Thomas had been at a wedding in Balmaclellan and, as it was at some distance from his mother's house, he had spent the night at the home of his uncle, Robert McLellan of Barscobe. While sleeping peacefully there he had been apprehended by a party of dragoons looking for his uncle. It must have been soon after this that Cornet Graham was passing by Barscobe Castle on a Sunday morning and saw Barscobe and two others run out of the house into the nearby wood. He followed them and captured them.

There is a record of Claverhouse escorting prisoners up to Edinburgh soon after 13th March 1682, the most important of which was Robert McLellan of Barscobe. He was to be hanged on 28th March, but offered to take the Test and appealed to the King for mercy. Clearly that was some time in coming and Barscobe had become worn down and disheartened by all his troubles and suffering, for on 22nd May he claimed he was sickly and if he was not released at least briefly he would likely 'fall into great illness'. His appeal for temporary release was rejected, though the Privy Council gave the Chancellor the authority if he felt Barscobe needed better air to send him instead to the Bass Rock or Blackness Castle. Finally a reprieve by the King came through on 12th July and he was allowed to go free, provided he made himself useful.

No doubt there was disappointment amongst the Covenanting extremists that he had abandoned the cause, though to what extent he 'made himself useful' to the authorities is unclear. Tragically he was to lose his life soon after. A false story later passed around that he had been strangled in his own house by an extremist because he had procured his liberation by signing the bond of peace. However James King Hewison in his 1913 book on the Covenanters tells the actual, equally tragic, story. In March 1684 the trial of the slayers of Robert McLellan of Barscobe took place in Edinburgh. The Judiciary Record records the following:

> 'Maclellan, Robert Grierson of Milnmark and William, his brother, after attending the funeral of the child of William Edgar [in Gordonstoun], retired to Barbara Gordon's tavern to drink, then adjourned to that of William McErval in the Clachan of Dalry to continue the entertainment. Barbara Gordon, who was then pregnant, wrathful and disappointed, arrived and volleyed out the most indecent language, especially against the wife of William Grierson. He retaliated with a blow which the delicate woman could ill stand, and the gallant Barscob resented, the latter in turn striking Grierson. Grierson seized the laird by the hair. Noses bled. In the brawl Barscob fell in the fire and sustained fatal injuries. The prosecution was at the instance of Elizabeth Logan, widow of Barscob, and her brother-in-law James Maclellan of Sundaywell, against the two Griersons and John Henrysone. The jury acquitted the prisoners and found that Barscob was subject to epileptic fits, and had beaten the accused.'

Thus ended the life of one who had dedicated his life to the Covenanting cause, but in the end found the cost and sacrifice too heavy to bear.

JOHN MALCOLM OF DALRY

John Malcolm, a young weaver from Dalry village, was captured after the Battle of Bothwell Bridge in 1679 and incarcerated in the Covenanters' prison in Greyfriars churchyard in Edinburgh. He was one of the 257 prisoners remaining from the original 1200 imprisoned there in inhumane conditions; the authorities decided to sell them into slavery in the English plantations in America. However the ship was wrecked at Deerness in the Orkney Islands in late 1679 and only around 50 of them survived. Malcolm was among them. He must have managed to escape back to the south-west, for six months later he was captured in the skirmish at Ayrsmoss and shortly after executed in the Grassmarket at Edinburgh. We know little more of his story, but we do have a lengthy 'Dying Testimony' that he read out at the scaffold on 13th August 1680 just before he died.

His dying testimony is reproduced in *A Cloud of Witnesses*, compiled by John Thomson in 1871, which can be accessed on the internet. I will include some of it here, for it helps give us a picture of the man and the times he lived in:

'I desire the audience of you, who are here spectators and auditors, to hear some words of a dying man, ready to offer up this tabernacle in your sight. I would have it among my last wishes, that you would consider your ways and your doings, that are not good; and not harden your hearts as in the provocation; for ye have to do with an holy God, who is quickly about to come, in flaming fire, to take vengeance on all the ungodly profane persons who are living at ease in Zion, and rejoicing in the afflictions of the people of God…. But this is ground of encouragement to the seekers of God; that He is keeping up a party in the land that see it their duty to contend for His cause and interest, and shall overcome through the blood of the Lamb, and by the word of their testimony; who are not loving their lives unto the death, to contend for His cause and interest….

The Lord determined me to join myself with that party, and I do not repent it this day. I count it my duty, and no sin nor rebellion. I think it my credit to serve such a noble Master; and, indeed, I wonder at His condescendency, that ever He sought service from such a wretched sinner as I have been, who lived a stranger to Him all my days. But, O wonderful love! Oh! I wonder at the matchless acts of the Lord's condescendency and incomprehensible ways with me! that He has made choice of such a poor, weak, frail pickle of dust as I am, and has led me out and in, and has brought me to this place of execution to give my testimony to His work, cause, and interest; and has passed by the eminent, wise, and prudent in the land, and has made choice of such a feckless nothing as I am. But blessed be His glorious name, that will have His word made out, that out of the mouth of babes and sucklings He can perfect His praise….

[*He had been accused of being with Richard Cameron's band from April until June.*] I was but two days with them, intending no other thing but to hear the Gospel, and for this I suffer; I bless the Lord, not as an evil doer, but for my duty; for ye know we are all bound in covenant, both Kirk and State, according to the Coronation-oath, and the Covenants were owned and sworn, both by the supreme magistrate, the nobles, gentry, and commons of all sorts. The Lord did wonderfully shine upon this land, so that it became the glory of the whole world; the fame of it went abroad, and was renowned through the nations. I have heard, that if a stranger of another kingdom had come into a church in this land, there was such a frame of spirit among the people, that the stranger would have thought that they had been all saints. The Church then was fair as the moon, clear as the sun, and terrible as an army with banners. But we have not been content with these days. Then the swearer was bound up from oaths, and the drunkard's throat ran dry; iniquity stopped her mouth. The Lord was with His people in those days; the Gospel was successful.

And yet I can say, there have been as great days of the Gospel in the west of Scotland in the foresaid months, in the fields, as were in Scotland, since it was Scotland. I am sure, the Gospel preached by Mr. Richard Cameron especially was backed with the power and presence of Christ. As much of Christ and heaven were found, as finite creatures on earth were able to hold, yea, and more than they could hold; the streams of the living waters ran through among His people at these meetings, like a flood upon the souls of many, who can witness, if they were called to it, that they would not have been afraid of ten thousands; 'The shout of a king was heard among them.'

The fruits of it, I am hopeful, shall appear after this; all the troopers and dragoons in the three kingdoms, will never get that fire of love quenched that is kindled in the breasts of some in that country; it will never be quenched. It will not rot; the fathers will be telling the children of it, when they are old men, who are not taken away with the wrath that is coming on, to avenge the quarrel of a broken Covenant. They will be telling, that 'in the year 1680 there were as great days, as there are now; when there were prelates through these lands, upon the mountains up and down this west; it was then that I got on the zeal of God upon my soul.' And they shall say, 'Who were they that preached in mosses and mountains, and not in the kirks nor houses? Did not all the godly ministers, when the apostate prelates were in the land, go out and witness and testify against them, with their lives in their hands?'…

So I am not in the dark, how and for what I suffer. I am clear that I was in my duty, and I have peace in it since, and I grow still clearer in it; glory to His name; for it is true that after I got my indictment and received my sentence, I wanted the countenance of God; for I never knew that the Lord loved me, but since that time; but I was never in the dark about the righteousness of the cause. I knew it would bear a suffering unto blood and death. And now, I am clear of my interest, and clear as to the grounds that I am laying down my life for this day. I could wish that every hair of my head were a life for His sake, and His persecuted cause….

And because of that mistake, which they say in my indictment — that Presbyterians, and I amongst the rest, had cast off all fear of God and are against all good order and civil law; I declare I adhere to kingly government, but not to perjury and tyranny, turning upside down Church and State, contrary to the word of God, our Covenants, and the laws of the nation, and contrary to the declaration at Dunfermline, the coronation-oath, and the acts of general assembly, and acts of Parliament ratifying Presbytery, and abjuring this prelatic hierarchy, which is now re-established, and Presbytery rescinded….

I no sooner began to look to Him but He made me welcome, and put me to work, though I be but young, and know nothing. He was tender of me. He took me to Bothwell Bridge to own His cause; and I had many temptations to stay; what from my mother, and from one hand and another; but I durst not for my soul stay behind. I thought it my duty to join myself with that party against the Lord's enemies, and the Lord was good to me there, many ways. He covered my head in the day of battle, and suffered not one hair of my head to fall to the ground, and He suffered many, better than me a thousand times, to fall on all hands of me. So I thought then I held my life of Him; and the Lord brought me to the Greyfriars Churchyard; though I came almost naked, yet He mounted me better than ever I was before with clothes, and wonderfully provided for me beyond many others. I bless the Lord, my mother's sickness did not keep me from Bothwell Bridge; and when I was in the Greyfriars Churchyard, I was threatened with death by the Justice-General, who swore a great oath that I should die if I would not take the Bond. I told him, as it was true, that many better than I had been hanged; but I was brought out of his hand, and the Lord took me to

Fig. 2: Dalry Church, with Gordon memorial stone in foreground.

Fig. 3: Memorial stone for Sir Alexander Gordon of Earlstoun.

the sea, and did deliver me from the ragings thereof, when He suffered many better to lose their lives. And when He laid His hand upon me by sickness, He made me to be favoured by all my enemies. He healed me, and brought me home, and then He called me out to hear the Gospel, for which I desire to bless Him, and within a little while I shall praise Him for it. The Lord was so seen amongst His persecuted handful there, that He did engage me to join with them, who were hazarding their lives upon the fields for Him. I was at that late engagement [Ayrsmoss], and the Lord took some work off my hand there, and has brought me to this place this day to lay down my life for His sake. And this is the last combat I shall have. I shall work no more; I shall suffer no more; I shall fear no more; I shall sin no more. I must take my leave of you all, and so rest in His love. I go where all tears shall be wiped away; where the servant is made free from his master; to the land where the inhabitants shall not say they are sick....

Join with His people, and cast in your lot with them, and do not stand on the other side; let His cause be your cause in weal and woe. O noble cause! O noble work! O noble heaven! O noble Christ, that makes it to be heaven! And He is the owner of the work. O noble Mediator of the new covenant! O noble Redeemer, who is powerful to help in time of need, and will help such as trust in Him! There was never one that trusted in Him that came to loss. He made them aye up, sometimes with an hundred-fold in this life, and heaven after. I lay down my life, not as an evil-doer, but as a sufferer for Christ....

I recommend my spirit to Him that is able to save to the uttermost all that come to Him through Christ, and desire to take my leave of all created comforts. Farewell all relations; farewell world; farewell sin! Welcome Christ, welcome heaven, and glory for evermore!"

4
DALRY CHURCHYARD

At the foot of Dalry village, or the 'auld clachan of Dalry' as it was often called, and close to the River Ken, stands Dalry Church surrounded by its graveyard. Alongside it to the north, and rising above it, the large castle motte bears testimony to an earlier time of warfare and troubles. A church stood here even in those distant times. Dalry churchyard has a number of connections with the Covenanters, and these are recounted below.

SIR ALEXANDER GORDON OF EARLSTOUN

The story of the Gordons of Earlstoun is covered in the chapter of this book on Earlstoun Castle. The following words are recorded on Alexander Gordon amongst the Gordon papers in the Ewart Library, Dumfries:

'He died at Airds 1726 and was buried in Dalry Churchyard, south side near the dyke, on which spot his grandson, Sir John Gordon intends raising a monument to his Memory with the following inscription:-

To the Memory of the very worthy Pillar of the Church of Scotland, Sir Alexander Gordon of Earlstoun, Bart., who after many years sufferings, died 1726, aged 76.

The following lines are inscribed by his Grandson, Sir John Gordon 178 : (full date missing)

Who e'er thou art whose steps are guided here,
Read and bestow a sigh, a silent tear,

Read sad vicissitudes of Grief and Woe
*   That wait the tragic scenes of life below.*
'Twas when the Brother's ruled with Anarch Sway
*   And reason hurri'd from the Throne away*
When Irreligion, Luxury and Waste
*   Expell'd reflection from the Sovereign's Breast*
'Mongst those whose bosom fir'd with ardent zeal
*   For Liberty's Cause and for the public weal*
In Earlstoun expiring virtue found
*   The firmest Patriot on deserted Ground*
Those sparks celestial fill'd his generous mind
*   For pure religion, not to forms confined*
Search Woodrow's faithful pages, there you'll find
*   How much he suffered, and how long confin'd*
How his lov'd father to tyrannick sway
*   And unrelenting Prelates fell a prey.*
Condemn'd and after try'd, unheard before
*   On Liberty's fair Isle, or distant shore*
Yet Providence whose Power omnific reigns
*   Preserv'd his life and humbl'd both the kings*
Pursue his steps and may it still inspire
*   And fill your soul with emulative fire.*
No more let slavery shake her galling chain
*   Nor Persecution wave her torch again.*
Surviv'd near forty years, the Cause sustain'd
*   The sufferer died and his Heav'n regained*
Without a tomb, till now forgot he lay
*   Yet still rever'd and ages worn away.'*

It is not known where exactly he was buried and sadly through lack of funds his grandson was never able to execute his plan to erect a stone over Alexander's grave inscribed with the words that he had composed. In 2011 however, some 240 years later, funds were raised to erect just such a stone and provide a fitting memorial to that worthy Covenanter. The stone was erected on the north side of the entrance to Dalry Session House (see Figs. 2 and 3). It doesn't include all the words of his poem; but then not all the words of the poem that John composed for his great-grandfather are included on the stone he did manage to erect in Glasford churchyard where William was buried.

DALRY COVENANTER MARTYRS

One notorious individual associated with Dalry was James McMichael. Though born at Dalzean on the Scar Water in Penpont parish, the brother of Daniel McMichael, who according to Simpson was a much more gentle and pious man who was also martyred for his faith, he is believed to have spent most of his youth at the Lorg in the far north of Dalry parish. James linked himself with the outlawed minister Richard Cameron, founder of the Cameronians, and signed the Sanquhar Declaration which was attached to the Mercat Cross in Sanquhar. Almost certainly he was involved in the skirmish with government forces at Ayrsmoss where Cameron was killed, and later he took part in the Enterkin attack where some Covenanter prisoners were set free. There are numerous Privy Council reports from 1684 of him roaming around with other rebels in the hills, seeking sustenance from those who would provide it. He was particularly outraged by those who informed on their brethren. One such informer trying to make his escape from a group of Covenanters, by the name of George Roan of Stroanpatrick, is said to have been felled by McMichael's thrown sword and bled to death of his injuries after a main artery in his leg was severed. Simpson records this incident in his book *Traditions of the Covenanters*. Though how true this is has to be doubted, as the Privy Council records of August 1684 name the killers as the fugitives William Herries, James McMillan and Robert Grierson.

But perhaps McMichael's most notorious deed was the killing of Peter Peirson, the curate of Carsphairn. This man had been directly responsible for the arrest and subsequent death or transportation of 21 local people and a group of supposedly unarmed Covenanters had gone to the manse in Carsphairn to demand that he sign a paper agreeing to desist from all further informing against his parishioners. He met two of them at the door, one of them being McMichael, with sword and pistol in hand, and called them inside. But when he heard their demand he flew into a rage and ushered them towards the door. As he did so James McMichael made a grab for him and in the ensuing scuffle Peirson was shot dead. McMichael claimed it was an accident, though others claimed he had actually taken his own pistol along secretly. Whatever the truth, McMichael was dismissed by Renwick and the Covenanting Societies from membership because he showed no remorse for what had happened and they were unwilling to countenance such a violent act.

Fig. 4: Covenanter stone, Dalry churchyard.

His reaction was to throw all caution to the wind. A week later he and seven others, at least three of the others besides McMichael from Dalry parish, forced an entry into Kirkcudbright Tolbooth and released the Covenanters held prisoner there, during which action a guard was killed. And two days later, on 18th December 1684, Claverhouse caught up with them on Auchencloy Moor, off the Raider's Road south of New Galloway at grid reference NX 603708. Two escaped, two were captured and later executed. The other four were killed.

Claverhouse in his Memoirs records that the Covenanters fought for their lives with sword and pistol, and Claverhouse himself, who prided himself in his skill with the sword, engaged McMichael in mortal combat. Claverhouse was so hard pressed by McMichael's superior swordplay that he had to call upon the help of a sergeant of dragoons who rushed on McMichael from behind and cleaved his skull with one blow. On hearing Claverhouse call for help, McMichael is said to have exclaimed: 'You dare not abide the issue of a single combat; and had your helmet been like mine, a soft bonnet, your carcass had ere this found a bed upon the heath.' After the fight was over McMichael lay dead upon the moss and Ferguson, Grierson and Stewart, who had all been badly wounded, were shot dead where they lay. Their bodies were left where they had fallen. It was there that their friends found them. Ferguson, who came from other parts, was buried where he lay; but the bodies of the other three were carried back to Dalry where they were buried by their families in the churchyard there. But no sooner had the graves been filled in than Claverhouse arrived with his troopers. They dug up the bodies and hung the corpses from a tree beside the church, and the villagers were ordered from their homes and forced to parade past them as a warning of what would happen to them if they supported the Covenanters. Stewart and Grierson's bodies they then allowed to be reburied, but in the northernmost corner of the churchyard, a place usually kept for thieves and moral outcasts. A flat tabletop stone lies over their graves (Fig. 4). The wording round the margin is as follows:

> Here lyeth Robert Stewart, son to Major Robert Stewart of
> Ardoch, and John Grierson, who was murdered by Graham
> of Claverhouse, Anno 1684, for their adherence to Scotland's
> Reformation and Covenants National and Solemn League.

In the centre is a poetic epitaph:

> Behold, behold, a Stone here's forced to cry,
> 'Come see two Martyrs under me that ly!'
> At water of Dee who slain were by the hand
> Of crual Claverhouse and's bloody band.
> No sooner had he done this horrid thing
> But's forc'd to cry Stewart's soul in Heaven doth sing.
> Yet strange his rage pursu'd even such when dead
> And in the tombs of their ancestors laid,
> Causing their Corps be raised out of the same,
> Discharging in church-yard to bury them.
> All this they did 'cause they would not perjure
> Our Covenants and reformation pure.
> Because, like faithful Martyrs, for to dy
> They rather chus'd than treacherouslie comply
> With cursed Prelacy, the Nation's bane,
> And with indulgencie our churches stain.
> Perjured intelligencers were so rife
> Shew'd their curs'd loyalty to take their life. Memento Mori.

Robert Stewart's parents are buried under a tabletop stone near
the Gordon burial aisle, the preserved roofless side-aisle of the
earlier pre-Reformation church. His father Major Robert Stewart of
Ardoch died in 1678. In 1620 Sir Robert Gordon of Lochinvar gave
a 120 year lease of the land of Ardoch to John Stewart of Manquhill,
Major Stewart's father. Manquhill is in the north-east of Dalry

parish, and Major Stewart seems to have lived at both Manquhill and Ardoch. In 1662 'Robert Stewart of Manquhill' was fined £1000 for his support of the Covenanting cause. (Interestingly Alexander Stewart of Physgill, who was shortly to become the 3rd Earl of Galloway, witnessed a bond for Major Stewart in February 1666 in Dalry, suggesting there was a family link with that influential family. Alexander's mother was an aunt of Robert Grierson of Lag, the arch-persecutor of the Covenanters - an example of the complex relationships of many of the landed gentry of the south-west of Scotland.) Major Stewart's older son James took over Ardoch on his father's death. Robert was his younger son and is recorded in the Fugitives' Roll of 1684 as living at Manquhill. Like James McMichael, he also signed the Sanquhar Declaration and took part in the Enterkin attack, and in the Privy Council records there are a number of accounts where he is named as one of the rebels roaming around the hills – often in the company of William Hunter of Dalry, who was one of the Covenanters captured at Auchencloy and executed a few days later at Kirkcudbright. John Grierson is probably the John Grier of Blackmark named on the Fugitives' Roll. But as for James McMichael's body, the villagers were forced to leave it hanging from the tree, swinging in the wind, for a further three days until some of his friends came under cover of darkness and spirited his body away to a safe resting place in the hills. It is said that his body was brought back to an unmarked grave in Dalry churchyard after the Settlement of 1689.

A sword was found hidden in a small building behind the Clachan Inn in Dalry when the former was being demolished in the 1960s (see Figs. 5a,b). Around 1970 local historian and archaeologist Alastair Penman took it to Dumfries Museum and from there it was transferred to the National Museum in Edinburgh. Apparently it is a Solingen steel blade, imported hilt-less into Scotland in a batch of 60 blades by Lord Kenmure. These were given to local Covenanters and each person put on their own hilt. There is a code of Roman numerals on both sides of the blade. This was decoded at

Figs. 5a and 5b: Sword believed to have belonged to James McMichael.

the museum to read 'James' on one side and 'Michael' on the other; the code is believed to have been based on the books of the New Testament, drilling down through book, chapter and verse to the words 'James' and 'Michael' (archangel). One then only has to add in 'Mc' to get the name of the probable owner of the sword, James McMichael.

It is probable that when the bodies of James McMichael and the other Covenanters killed at Auchencloy were found by their friends, the sword was lying there also and was brought back to Dalry with the bodies. There it must have lain hidden until it was found over 300 years later. It is now in the possession of Dalbeattie Museum.

REV WILLIAM BOYD

There is another stone with a Covenanting link in the churchyard. It is the tombstone for Rev William Boyd, minister of Dalry from 1690 to 1741. It is a tabletop stone located just south-east of the Newall mausoleum on the lower ground of the churchyard, and its Latin inscription is now difficult to read. Boyd had joined the Cameronians and fled to Holland during the persecution, where he became friendly with William of Orange and accompanied the prince to this country. On William's accession to the throne Boyd proclaimed him king at Glasgow Cross and shortly after was ordained minister in Dalry, where he was to serve as minister for over 50 years. Under the chapter on Balmaclellan there is a story recorded of a conventicle conducted by Rev Thomas Vernor on the top of the nearby Mulloch hill near the end of the time of troubles which Boyd also attended.

ADAM FORRESTER OF KNOCKSHEEN

I mention also the intriguing story of Adam Forrester of Knocksheen in Kells parish, on which Burns is believed to have based his poem 'Tam O'Shanter'. The story goes that Adam Forrester was making his way home on his horse one night when he heard the sound of music coming from Dalry Church. Looking in he saw the Clachan witches dancing away to wild music. He shouted out, in Tam O'Shanter style, to the local barmaid, "Ah, Lucky Hair, ye'll no deny this the morn!" and had barely time to mount his horse when they were out and after him. Up on the shoulder of Waterside Hill he realised they were catching up on him; so he jumped off his horse and drew a circle with his sword in the name of God around the place where he stood. And within that circle he and his horse were protected from attack - though in the encounter his horse lost its tail, which had been grabbed by one of the witches! When they heard a cock crow on a neighbouring farm, heralding daybreak, the witches suddenly departed. A few further embellishments to the story are recorded, one of which has the devil himself seated among the witches in the church. The 1849 OS map marks 'The Score' up on Waterside Hill where he is supposed to have been saved from his pursuers; and you can still see the oval shape of it, hollowed out slightly from the surrounding boggy ground at grid reference NX 605816. The first written record of this story and of 'the Score' is in a book published by Robert Trotter in 1822, in which he declares that for many years Captain Newall of Waterside and his brother Charles cleaned it out every Halloween morning and drank a cup of the best claret in their cellar in memory of Forrester the Dauntless!

I believe that story originates from Covenanting times. It's known that Grierson of Lag stabled his horses in Dalry Kirk and one can well believe that if he desecrated the church in that way he would have been more than likely to have encouraged the odd wild party or two in the church in those lawless times. To many local folk he was the devil incarnate. In the Gordon papers I came across mention of a financial bond granted in 1670 by Adam Forrester of Knocksheen and his mother Margaret to a member of the Gordon family. And intriguingly the Forrester family plot is right up by the side of Dalry Church. There are two what I assume must be later Adam Forresters from the same family buried there. Perhaps the original Adam Forrester was buried just where he looked in the window on that dramatic night. You wonder what kernel of truth there is at the heart of that strange tale!

5
EARLSTOUN CASTLE

Earlstoun Castle lies about two kilometres north of Dalry village. It is reached along a private road which passes near Earlstoun House and then continues on to the castle and a couple of private houses at the Byres of Earlstoun. It is fine for walkers to approach the castle along the private road, and the owners are comfortable for vehicles to drive up to the castle if the occupants find walking any distance difficult. Particularly striking is the Earlstoun oak, a fine old tree a hundred metres or so south of the castle and now near the end of its life, which features in the story below.

Earlstoun Castle dates from the late 16th or early 17th century and was built by the Gordons of Earlstoun (Fig. 6). Significant additions and improvements were made to the castle in 1655 by William Gordon and his wife Mary Hope, and a date stone with initials WG and MH was built into a two storey addition to the castle abutting the east gable. This part of the castle was demolished in 1950 and the date stone reset in the older, original part of the castle wall, where it can still be seen.

The Gordon family of Earlstoun were staunch supporters of the Covenanting cause. William Gordon of Earlstoun was a godly man who at one time had intended to train as a Church of Scotland minister. But when his older brother died young and then his father died he inherited the family estate. Mention has already been made of him in chapters 1 and 3. He was ordered in 1663, as patron, to present the Bishop's nominee to the parish of Dalry but refused. He was fined £3500 scots that same year for being a Presbyterian. In 1664 the Privy Council passed an act against him for attending local conventicles at which there were great numbers of people. He was heavily fined and eventually outlawed and orders given to

Fig. 6: Earlstoun Castle, with Earlstoun oak in foreground.

the soldiers to kill him whenever they met him. He fled to London for a time. After expressing disapproval of the Pentland Rising he was able to return home but he soon got into trouble again and in 1667 a military garrison under Sir William Bannatyne was sent to occupy the castle; he was compelled to hide in dens and caves to avoid the soldiers. It was at this time that he and his son Alexander are believed to have built a small hideout in the woods only about a quarter of a mile from Earlstoun Castle, carefully concealed in the densest thickets. There they hid on their own doorstep while the soldiers searched far and wide for them. It was a place where other Covenanters joined them also and they sought to encourage one another in the faith. The low stone walls of that simple dwelling are still to be seen in the woods (Fig. 7).

In the summer of 1678 the greatest conventicles of

Fig. 7: Remains of 'chapel' in Earlstoun wood.

Covenanting times were held in the parish of Irongray. People came from far and wide, even from Clydesdale, and one Sunday around 3000 people gathered for communion at Skeoch Hill. Three of Galloway's most respected outed ministers officiated – John Welsh of Irongray, John Blackadder of Troqueer and Samuel Arnot of Tongland. William Gordon was there with a large troop of Galloway horse, and there were also others there protecting the worshippers; but they found safety in numbers and the government troops did not trouble them. You can still see some of the stones used as communion tables on the hillside there.

In the end the injustices meted out to the people got to William. He was incensed at the way the unjust laws were rigorously enforced and the way people at all levels of society were oppressed – robbed of their lives, their liberty and of their possessions. He felt the situation called for his leadership in standing up for those who were oppressed and had no voice; and reluctantly he felt the situation now called for a more extreme remedy. In June 1679, having raised some forces he sent them north with his son Alexander, but under strict orders that they should not engage with the government forces. Meanwhile he stayed behind to settle his affairs, which took much longer than he had intended. He had hoped to avoid bloodshed by engaging in dialogue with the Duke of Monmouth and by that means reach some compromise.

He arrived too late. He was just past Strathaven and about six miles from Bothwell Bridge, when he began to meet Covenanters fleeing from the Battle of Bothwell Bridge who could give him no clear information. As he bravely continued on, he was met by a party of dragoons who shot him dead on his hesitating to surrender. His two servants, John Ramsay and John Tilly, gave themselves up and later returned to Dalry where they lived a further forty years. His corpse was retrieved and buried in the churchyard of Glassford by the orders of Lady Harper, his wife's sister, who had always held him and his family in the highest esteem.

His son Alexander was no less noted a Covenanter. He escaped from the Battle of Bothwell Bridge and as he was riding through Hamilton he was recognised by a man who had formerly been his cooper and a tenant of his. This man immediately made him dismount and buried his saddle and horse harness in a dunghill. He then made him enter the cottage and put on women's clothes and when the king's troops arrived a few moments later and began searching every home he was quietly rocking a baby's cradle. Shortly after he carefully made his way home to Earlstoun, probably under cover of darkness. Only a day or two later the castle was surrounded by some of Claverhouses's dragoons and he only just had time to hide himself behind the ceiling boards of a room immediately above the kitchen. His wife and family and friends recognised that it wasn't safe for him to stay at home and four days after the Battle of Bothwell Bridge Alexander and his wife slipped away to Holland. He was outlawed and his lands forfeited, though it wasn't until 1686 that his estates were actually sold.

He may have stayed a year or so in Holland, but he later returned to Scotland, where he lay low to avoid capture. For a time troops were billeted in Earlstoun Castle and when they were absent he sometimes returned to sleep in his own bed, only quick actions enabling him to elude capture on a number of occasions. A hundred metres south of the castle is the Earlstoun oak (see Fig. 6). Now it is but a shadow of its former glory, barely hanging on to life; but in Alexander's time it was a large stately oak amongst the leafy limbs of which he sought refuge a number of times, hiding there when he wasn't able to get further away on hearing of the approach of soldiers - and then escaping to a safer place when night fell. A young oak grown from an acorn harvested from the old tree in 2003 can be seen between the tree and the castle.

One memorable story concerning Alexander is of the time he was warned that soldiers were on their way and, realising he had no time to escape, he quickly changed into the clothes of a working man. He was busy chopping wood in the courtyard of the castle helped by a female servant when the soldiers rode up. The commander asked the wood-cleavers if Earlstoun was within and, when he replied 'no' he was asked to throw down his axe and join in the search. He complied obediently and seemed to enter into the search of the castle as heartily as the soldiers themselves. When they couldn't find Alexander they asked their guide if he knew where his master's hiding place was in the woods. Not wanting to lie, he replied, referring to another Master, Jesus Christ. His Master, he said, had no hiding place that he knew of; and he was certain that if he understood that any person was seeking Him, He would show Himself before very long!

In Covenanting circles Alexander was recognised as one who could do much to further their cause because of his education and standing in society. They were particularly concerned at the way their cause was being vilified abroad and recognised the need for someone to speak on their behalf against all the falsehoods being circulated about them. They also recognised the need to find safe havens to which the brethren whose lives were most in danger could escape for a while; or if that were too difficult to at least raise some funds overseas to help support them in their times of desperate need. James Renwick, in a letter sent to him at Earlstoun, invited Alexander to a General Meeting of the Covenanting Societies in Edinburgh in April 1682 where he was given a commission to represent them abroad in just these matters. He took up this task with dedication. Just over a year later in June 1683 he was on a ship bound for Holland from Newcastle with his servant, both under false names, when others on board became suspicious of their true identity. Suspecting he was about to be arrested he threw his papers into the sea. Unfortunately he was observed doing this, and the papers were retrieved and he was arrested. He and his servant were transferred up to Edinburgh to the Tolbooth in the Royal Mile, where he was subjected to intense questioning. But they could find nothing to fix on him with regard to the Rye House plot, with which in fact he had had no involvement. On 12th July his servant – Edward Aitkin from Crawfordjohn – was condemned to be hanged for supporting him knowing him to be an outlawed man; and eight days later he was hanged in the Grassmarket.

On 21st August Alexander himself was sentenced to be beheaded at the Cross of Edinburgh on 29th September, but before that to be subjected to torture to try and extract any information possible from him before he died. That same day he wrote a letter to Secretary Middleton asking him to consult with his Majesty's Advocate, then in London, as to whether it was consistent with the law of Scotland that he should be tortured when under sentence of death. The answer came back that indeed it was permissible. And so an illustrious committee was appointed to meet with him to cross-examine him on 25th September. On seeing the instruments of torture all at the ready, Alexander managed to persuade them that he would be able to give them a more measured and full response to their questions if he wasn't subjected to torture, to which they acquiesced. All his answers to these questions are preserved and can be read. But they didn't satisfy His Majesty's Court in London, who put out an Express Order for Alexander to be put to the torture on 23rd November. As he was about to be tortured he was thrown into such a wild fury that he terrified the whole courtroom, and led to him being given the nickname 'The Bull of Earlstoun'.

On the advice of the doctor he was sent to Edinburgh Castle for a change of air and to allow time for the whole case against him to be better appraised. There on the 7th December, with his health very poor and thinking he was a dying man, he affirmed again his innocence of any plot against the king and affirmed the truth of the answers he had already given to their questions. Thankfully his health began to improve a little and his death sentence was postponed. His appeal for pardon began to make its way through the system. Meanwhile because of his fragile health he was sent to the Bass Rock in May 1684 for the sea air. He was there for the summer, after which he was transferred to Blackness Castle near Bo'ness in September. He remained there until the Glorious Revolution in 1689. When the prison doors were flung open on 5th January 1689 he refused to stir out of his room in the middle tower until he had entered a formal protest before witnesses to his wrongful imprisonment.

Through the financial help of family and friends he was able to return to his estate at Earlstoun in May 1690 with his wife and presumably his family. And there he lived out the rest of his days in quiet retirement from the affairs and politics of the day, until he finally died in 1726 aged 76. It has to be said that his treatment over the last years of his imprisonment can't have been too bad, as his wife was with him on the Bass Rock and at Blackness Castle and one of his children was actually born while they were both held in Blackness Castle. But he was a man who stood true to his Christian principles and was not prepared to compromise on matters he saw as important. And he did suffer much for the stand that he took.

The Gordons of Earlstoun never really recovered financially from the effects of the troubles and were forced to give up their estate in 1744.

It was Alexander's younger brother William who obtained the baronetcy for his services to the crown in 1706, and it was only in 1718 when he died with no heirs that the title of 'Sir' came to Alexander. We owe the inscription on Alexander's tombstone to his grandson Sir John Gordon. A handsome Doric pillar had been erected over the body of Alexander's father William in Glassford churchyard, but without any inscription, as the times wouldn't allow it. It was some 90 years later that John discovered that the stone was close to tumbling down and sought financial support from the line of the family that had inherited the estate towards its repair. He found no interest in his plans; and despite the poor state of his own finances he determined to press ahead anyway. In 1772 he had the monument dismantled and the stones renewed with additions, then rebuilt on a firmer foundation of a red tablestone from Cumberland. To this renewed monument was added an inscription entirely of his own composing. In September 2011 a conventicle was held there, a plaque dedicated to William and a young oak sapling planted there and blessed, grown from an acorn from the Earlstoun oak.

John also prepared a similar inscription for a stone for his grandfather Alexander, who had been buried in Dalry churchyard, on the south side by the dyke, but without a stone over his grave. Sadly his financial straits never allowed him to realise his plans. But his planned inscription was recorded in the Gordon papers held in the Ewart library in Dumfries; and in 2011, some 240 years later, a stone was raised to Alexander's memory in Dalry churchyard with this very inscription (see Ch.3).

THE 'CHAPEL IN THE WOODS'

The six inch Ordnance Survey map of 1849 marks a ruined chapel in Earlstoun wood, and I came across a fascinating passage in Simpson's 1841 book *Traditions of the Covenanters*. He writes,

'William Gordon was the proprietor of Earlstoun in the persecuting times. His covenanting principles rendered him obnoxious to the ruling party, and accordingly his house was made a garrison for Bannatyne and his troopers. The worthy man, being expelled from his own dwelling, constructed for himself a hiding-place in the deep and impenetrable thickets in the vicinity of the mansion-house, in which on many occasions he found a secure retreat. It does not appear that the resort was ever discovered by the enemy during the years of careful search that was made for the obnoxious members of that household. The existence of such a place was rumoured by tradition among the people of the neighbourhood, but no person could tell where it was. Its discovery, however, was made of late years by an inhabitant of the village of Dalry, who was one day searching the woods not far from the castle. It is a small narrow building, in the heart of the thickest and most impervious underwood and, even at the present time, when the forest is much less dense than it must formerly have been, is almost undiscoverable. Here, in this secrecy, did the worthy William Gordon and his son Alexander, the companion of his sufferings, often hide themselves in the day of peril; and this was the oratory in which many fervent prayers were addressed to the throne of grace by these sufferers for conscience' sake.'

The OS Name Book compiled to accompany the 1849 map says of the 'Old Chapel', 'It is said to have been erected by Gordon of Earlstoun after the period of the Scottish persecution in 1668 to commemorate the spot where the ejected Minister of the parish and his congregation had often met for public worship, hence the name Old Chapel.' That may be so, but the likelihood is that it was originally built by Gordon as a hideout and through much of the Covenanting times it was invaluable as a place to lie low and avoid the patrolling dragoons. I managed to locate the ruins of the building in 2003 at grid reference NX 61415 84222 (see Appendix 2). To reach it take the track to the east of the Earlstoun oak through the gate and then through a further gate into the wood. Follow the track round until just before it emerges into an area where commercial forestry has fairly recently been harvested. Just before leaving the old oak forest head off to the left of the track and about 100 metres into the wood you will find the ruins under a large horse chestnut tree (Fig. 7).

Local poet and farmer John Gordon Barbour of Bogue published a poem on the ruined chapel entitled 'Verses in the Chapel in Earlstoun Wood' in his book *Lights and Shadows of Scottish Character and Scenery* (p.345) published in 1824. He writes:

> Thy little walls in ruin lie –
> The hazel grows within thy porch –
> Yet faith and fervour here grew high –
> God dwelt in thee, thou sylvan church!
>
> The small birds joined the morning psalm –
> The blackbird join'd the evening hymn;
> And Heaven here shed the holy calm,
> When Suffering's cup ran to the brim.
>
> Sweet smelled the birch at dewy dawn:
> The milk-white thorn with beauty glow'd;
> Around thee skipt the simple fawn; -
> Thy floor the daisy-pranked sod.
>
> The haunted Ken ran murm'ring by;
> Far to the south spread thickest wood:
> Embosom'd there, yon turrets high
> Contain'd the patriot and the good.
>
> Yes – Earlstoun's tow'rs rose sweet beneath;
> And Gordon's race were owners there:
> They fought for Covenanter's faith –
> They rear'd thee – sylvan house of pray'r.

Earlstoun Castle

And in thy little rustic walls,
(Where carve or image ne'er were seen,
Nor column, nor rich capitals)
Have hordes of persecuted been.

And here hath Vernor raised the psalm,
And here hath Peden op'd the word,
And here was pour'd the heavenly balm
To soothe for persecution's sword!

Nor only when the leaf was green,
Nor only when strong summer glow'd,
But when rough winter snow'd the scene,
The hunted faithful sought their God.

And aye they wept, and aye they pray'd;
And aye they crav'd for help on high
To meet the savage Grierson's raid,
And Clavers' bloody troop defy.

For wicked Bannatyne would brag
How "Gordon's race he would cut up."
And when he went, the savage Lagg
Presented little kindlier cup.

These days are gone: yes – let them go;
The 'Stuart' horde have got their doom;
And shall lukewarmness reign below?
Shall luxury take the 'Cov'nant's' room?

Ah no! tho' low thy ruins lie –
Tho' now the grass grows in thy porch –
Let faith and fervour yet grow high;
God dwelt in thee – thou sylvan church!

6
BLACKWATER

The Black Water is a dramatic stream more reminiscent of a Highland burn. To reach it take what is called the 'High Carsphairn road', the minor road that heads northwards from the upper part of Dalry village. When one reaches the bridge over the Black Water you will see it tumbling down a ravine on the west side of the bridge. To the east the ground is more open, but the peaty water still cascades over a number of attractive waterfalls.

John Dempster lived at Garryaird, on the moor a little north of the Black Water in Dalry parish. You can read the results of my research into the Dempster family in Chapter 2. Traces of the house are visible on aerial photos at grid reference NX 628893, but there is very little to see on the ground. Dempster was present at the Battle of Bothwell Bridge and his strong Covenanting loyalties meant that he was remorselessly hounded by the troops over a number of years. Simpson in his 1841 book *Traditions of the Covenanters* tells his story well and I will allow him to tell it in his own words. I think it also gives a flavour of how writers in the first half of the nineteenth century romanticised the tales of the Covenanters:

'John Dempster, the Covenanter, lived at Garryaird, in the parish of Dalry, in Galloway. He followed the occupation of a tailor, and was one of the patriots who fought at Bothwell Bridge. Being a noted non-conformist, a strict search was frequently made for him in the district where he resided. So intent were his enemies on his apprehension, that he was obliged to leave his house, and to seek an abode in the woods and caves in the neighbourhood. He selected a hiding-place in the rugged side of the Black Water, a stream which empties itself into the silvery Ken a few miles above the village of Dalry. The cave of the rock in which he lodged was the place where, in the summer months, he plied his trade, while his wife conveyed his food to him by stealth.

On one occasion his wife, in the evening dusk, had brought him a supply of provisions, and having learned that the enemy was not in the neighbourhood, she persuaded him to leave his retreat, and to seek shelter for one night under his own roof. The worthy man was induced to visit his household in the hope that he might be permitted to remain for a few hours in his own lowly hut without interruption, and then to return in the morning to his rocky cell. The night, accordingly, was spent without the intrusion of the military, and John, after the morning's repast, and after the accustomed family devotions, was preparing to return to his hiding-place by the purling brook. It was a fine morning; and his wife, whose solicitude for her husband's welfare was incessant, went to the front of the house to ascertain if the space within the field of her vision was clear of the wandering troopers, who were frequently abroad at all seasons seeking to surprise the helpless and unwary. As she cast her anxious eye afar over the landscape, she noticed a band of dragoons marching at their utmost speed in the direction of the house. The unwelcome tidings were communicated to John, who lost not a moment in making his escape. As he was running at his full speed, having thrown off his shoes to facilitate his flight, he was observed by the horsemen, who pursued him hotly, and fired several times without effect.

John fled in the direction of Earndarrock Wood, a thicket about the distance of half a mile from his house. Between him and the wood there lay a moss, or space of boggy ground, which suddenly arrested the progress of the dragoons when they approached it. One of their number, however, found his way around by the end of the morass, and furiously spurring his war-steed, came up to John as he was attempting to scramble over the dyke that surrounded the wood. He had no weapons of defence; but remembering that he had with him the large scissors which were employed in cutting the good broad cloth, he drew them from his pocket, and just when the horse had come so close that he felt its head rubbing and pressing on his shoulder, he drove the sharp-pointed instrument into the animal's forehead with the force of desperation. The violent stroke made the horse rear and spring to the one side, so that his rider, who had uplifted his sword to strike, was cast impetuously on the ground. This overthrow afforded John time to dart into the wood before the party reached the spot. The troopers, leaving their horses at the edge of the wood, pursued him on foot to the brink of a deep ravine, down the rugged sides of which he made his way with all possible haste. His pursuers, finding it inconvenient to descend after him, employed themselves in tumbling large fragments of rock after him; but John escaped unhurt, and having reached the opposite side of the ravine, concealed himself among the bushes.

His wife witnessed the pursuit from the door of her house with intense anxiety. It is impossible to describe her feelings at the moment she saw the dragoon reach him, before he succeeded in entering the wood. But when she observed the fall of the trooper and perceived her husband running into the thicket, her hope revived. Her fears, however, were renewed when she saw the party dismount and dive into the wood, hunting among the trees and yelping like bloodhounds after their prey.

In a short time they emerged from the plantation, and returned to the house, where the afflicted wife and children were lamenting the loss of the husband and the father. The disappointed troopers declared that they had killed the rebel in the ravine, and had left his mangled body among the underwood. They enjoyed a malignant satisfaction in lacerating the good woman's feelings to the uttermost, who had no difficulty in believing their assertions respecting the murder. Such incidents were of daily occurrence, and the death of John was considered as nothing new nor incredible. The soldiers, on witnessing the excessive affliction of the family, wrought all manner of mischief, eating and drinking at their will, and destroying what they could not use.

When the troopers were gone, the household gave vent without restraint, to sincere and uncontrollable sorrow. "Come, my children," said the mother, "let us go into the wood and seek the bleeding body of your father, who has fallen by the hands of these cruel men, as an honoured witness for Jesus Christ." The dragoons were now out of sight, and they supposed that nothing was to be dreaded from them, as they had declared they had now perpetuated the murder they had so long sought to accomplish. The sun was now advancing to his meridian height; and the family, a weeping company, was preparing to traverse the wood in every direction, when a new thought struck the mother in a moment, and she stood still and considered. "My dear children," said she, "it has occurred to me that this account of your father's death by the dragoons is probably, after all, a mere fabrication of their own, to serve a purpose. Perhaps your father yet lives, and is in safety in some undiscovered hiding-place in the ravine; and the object of these unprincipled men may be to send us in search of him whom they could not find, and then to trace our steps and capture him. No trust can be put in the statements of these men; and perchance there is a snare laid to entrap us." It was exactly as the honest woman thought; the troopers invented the story for the purpose of imposing on the simple-hearted cottagers, that through their means they might the more easily accomplish their purpose.

Still it was a matter of uncertainty; and the surmises of

the mother, though amounting to a high probability, were not fully satisfactory, and the afflicted household earnestly longed for the shadows of the evening. John, in his cavern, was greatly solicitous about his family. He knew that the soldiers would be chagrined and exasperated at the disappointment they had met with, and that, therefore, they might vent their fury on his helpless wife and children. He durst not move from his retreat so long as the light of day continued, lest his enemies should be lying in wait in the skirts of the wood, ready to shoot or apprehend him on his first appearance. With impatient look he watched the progress of the descending sun, that under the cloud of night he might steal cautiously to his cottage to see how matters stood there, and to impart the joyful intelligence of his safety. As the distressed inmates of the cottage were making preparation for an immediate departure to the wood, the sound of footsteps was heard at the door, and the object of their solicitude stood before them. The surprise and the gladness of the household was indescribable; the affectionate wife fainted in her husband's arms, being overpowered by the strength of her emotions, and the children were bathed in tears of joy. The state of matters was fully rehearsed on both sides, and the liveliest gratitude was expressed to the great Preserver of life by this pious company.

As John's place of concealment within the precincts of the wood was now known to the enemy, it was obvious that they would not cease to frequent the spot till they finally succeeded in their object; and therefore it was agreed that he should seek a place of shelter in another quarter. There was an intimate friend of his, a sufferer in hiding, who had a cave in a hill above New Galloway, and to this man our worthy resolved to pay a visit. He accordingly left his family for a season – went in quest of his friend – found him in his hiding-place, and was warmly received by him.

He had not long remained here till he received information that a strict search was to be made on the mountain by the soldiers, who, it was supposed, were conducted by a spy who seemed to have some notion of the hiding-place. On receiving this friendly caution, John and his friend left the cave to seek concealment elsewhere. As they were traversing the hill they observed a company of troopers, who, guided by an informer, were coming directly to the cavern which they had just abandoned. They now plainly perceived that the warning they had received was not without ground, and that their only security lay in the speed of their flight. The dragoons, who by this time had them fully in their view, commenced a vigorous pursuit. The fugitives directed their course towards Loch Ken, a beautiful sheet of water which stretches along the valley, in the line of the river Ken, below New Galloway. They next turned in the direction of Balmaclellan, and were about to ascend the little eminence that leads to the village, when they perceived that they were out of their enemies' view; and seizing the advantage, they turned to a ravine in the Garple Glen, at a short distance from the place where they were, in which they had formerly found shelter, and which had been a place of retreat to many a wanderer in those fearful times. They reached the cave in safety; and the troopers arrived in Balmaclellan, where they searched every house in which they supposed the men might have taken refuge, but without success, and they were obliged to return to their quarters without their prey.

…

But though John Dempster escaped for a while from his cruel enemies, he gained at last the martyr's crown. One day when he was returning in the evening twilight from his place of concealment, he was met by a party of Lagg's men on Knockgree Hill, as they were returning to their garrison in the vicinity of the persecutor's residence. John descended the mountain, closely pursued by his enemies, and crossed the Water of Deuch. The gloom of the evening, however, and the dark heath over which he was fleeing, perplexed his enemies, and in their bewilderment they lost his track. They rode round and round, backward and forward, in expectation of stumbling upon him in some lurking-place, but were disappointed, and obliged to abandon their search. John sped to the lofty mountain of Craighit, where he found shelter for the night among the crevices of the rocks. Craighit was not a proper place for persons in John's condition, as it was in the full view of Garryhorn, Lagg's residence; and had it not been that he was greatly fatigued and overpowered, and perhaps sickly, he never would have allowed the light of day to dawn on him in this situation. Next morning Lagg was at the head of his troopers for the purpose of searching for wanderers in the neighbourhood. He had his eye on Craighit, and thinking that he saw an object in the distance, he brought his telescope to assist his vision, and by this means he obtained a distinct view of John cowering behind a rock on the hill. On this welcome discovery he instantly divided his men into two companies – the one made a circuit to the south, and the other to the west, with a view to circumvent the fugitive. John saw their movements, and instantly left his last place of shelter on earth. The scene of the pursuit was in full view of the people of Carsphairn, who looked on with absorbing interest, and with deep sorrow, to see the worthy man pursued like a partridge on the mountain. He left Craighit, crossed the Garry Burn, and hastened to reach the Bow Hill, with the intention of going down the back part of it into Loch Doon, if perchance he might there find another hiding-place.

The dragoons were pursuing with the utmost eagerness, and as hilariously as if they had been in keen chase after a furtive reynard [fox]. Lagg stood below in sight of his men, where he had a full view of all that was passing on the hill; and when, owing to the inequalities of the ground, the soldiers lost sight of the object of their pursuit, he made signs to them, and pointed out the direction in which they were to follow. When John reached the Bow Hill, he became fully aware of his situation, and saw that it was impossible to escape, as his pursuers were just at hand. He gained the height, however, and ran along it for a considerable distance to a point called Meaul Hill. Here the dragoons in two divisions met and closed him in. He was now entirely in the power of his ferocious enemies, who exulted in their success as joyously as if they had seized the richest prize. The poor captive, panting and exhausted, was allowed no time to kneel on the heath in prayer, nor to commit his soul formally to Him in whose presence he was about to appear as a sufferer in His cause. But though this favour was not granted, he was not unprepared. He had sought the Saviour before, and he had found Him, and now he was ready when called on to die in defence of His truth. His capture and death were almost instantaneous, for the merciless troopers shot him dead on the spot.

Thus fell a good man, who had endured many hardships and braved many storms of persecution for a number of years. He died an honoured witness for Christ, and sincerely lamented by the worthy people of the district in which he was known.'

I believe I managed to locate Dempster's hideout on the north side of the Black Water a little downstream from its nearest point to Garryaird, at grid reference NX 62378855 or What3Words frightens.pollution.pelting (see Appendix 2). Perhaps not exactly a cave, but a well camouflaged hollow on the edge of the river, with a small rowan tree growing above it (see Figs. 8, 9) – standing above it you're quite unaware of its existence. Perhaps a little damp at times,

Fig. 8: Proposed location of Dempster's hideout on the Black Water.

and rather wetter in the winter; but if he had made a little platform with sticks to raise himself a few inches and covered it with bracken he could have had quite a cosy den in which to ply his trade as a tailor. It is most likely that when he was surprised by the troopers he sought refuge in the ravine into which the Black Water descends to the west of the road. To find this hideout park by Blackwater Bridge on the B7000 and follow the sign on the north side of the bridge saying 'Path Butterhole Bridge 1½'. The hideout is about half a mile up this path.

I was curious also to find the cave that Simpson mentions on the Garple Burn and at first had no success. The burn passes through a dramatic ravine and it is easy to see that it would have been a perfect place for Covenanters to hide. Its steep wooded slopes descend to a river choked with many fallen trees and it is far from easy to make one's way upstream. Then I heard of others who knew

Fig. 9: Close up of Dempster's possible hideout.

of a cave and renewed my efforts. A little upstream from Holme House, and on the opposite side of the burn, I came across a cave in 2015 at grid reference NX 643799 only a few feet above the normal river level (Fig. 10). It is not a natural cave but an old mining adit or passageway extending into the hillside. With a head torch I was able to explore it to its end and a month or so later I went back with my sons and measured its length. It is about 29 metres long and I was just able to stand up in it, so it is a sizeable passageway. There is some standing water in the first part of it, but then it becomes drier though still damp. It would have been an excellent place to hide, though not the most comfortable. But further research has revealed that this mining adit would not have been there at the time of the Covenanters. It was almost certainly opened up during

Fig. 10: Cave on the Garple Burn.

the 1840s when, after the discovery of the Woodhead lead mine at Carsphairn, further exploration for mineral deposits was taking place in the area. But the adit follows an iron-mineralised shear zone and a point of weakness in the rock; so it is very likely that there was a small cave at the time of the Covenanters and that the miners tunnelled back from it into the hillside. This may indeed be the cave that Simpson refers to – and it would have been very hard for the troops to discover.

It is well worth taking a walk along the north side of the ravine above the main Castle Douglas road, peering down into its depths from time to time; or to approach it along the road to Grennan Mill, where an old stone bridge crosses the burn just above where a waterfall cascades down into the ravine.

The more adventurous and hardy might also like to climb

Fig. 11: View of Garryhorn from Carsphairn village. Meaul is just outside the photo, to the left on the skyline.

up to the place where Dempster was shot dead. To do so one needs to walk up past Garryhorn to the NW of Carsphairn (Fig. 11). On the way you may wish to visit the rocky outcrops on Craighit (NX 533928) and try to imagine where Dempster may have hid that night. Continue on then to the summit ridge of the Rhinns of Kells and about a kilometre north of the summit of Meaul Hill at grid reference NX 500917, some 50 metres to the west of the path along the ridge, you will find a small irregular upright stone with a brass plaque alongside it marking the place where tradition says that Dempster met his death (Figs. 12, 13).

A few years ago when exploring on the far side of the Rhinns of Kells I came across the ruins of a simple building above the forestry high up on the west flank of Coran of Portmark at grid reference NX 502944. It's not marked on any maps and is a very isolated spot, and I can't help wondering if it might also have been a Covenanter refuge. Perhaps it was to that place that Dempster was heading when the troops caught up with him. That whole wilderness area would have been a natural place for the Covenanters to seek

Fig. 12 (above): Dempster's grave on Meaul.
Fig. 13 (below): Plaque marking Dempster's grave.

refuge. It could be just a shepherd's summer shieling, but it is also possible that it has links further back to the time of the Covenanters.

7
UPPER HOLM OF DALQUHAIRN

There are a number of places on the fringes of the Glenkens that are well worth visiting. It is a long drive north into the heart of the hills to reach the Holm of Dalquhairn and the Lorg near the source of the Water of Ken, but one reaches at the end a little oasis of arable fields which I suspect has changed very little since the time of the Covenanters.

In 2017 we held a conventicle at the Upper Holm of Dalquhairn to remember John Fraser, who lived there with his wife Marion Howatson. Simpson records the trials he faced in his book *Traditions of the Covenanters.*

For many precious years John Fraser had enjoyed the ministry of John Semple, the charismatic minister of Carsphairn. Fraser was a man of great piety and deep Christian faith, and that made him stand firm in those troubled times as one who would not compromise his beliefs for a more formal expression of the faith which he believed lacked passion and heart. He wanted to be true to his Saviour. Between his home and the church dwelt Robert Cannon, the laird of Muirdrochwood - in those days pronounced Muirdrogat or Mondrogat. They had been companions in their youth, sitting together in Carsphairn Church under the ministry of Semple, but Simpson in his book *Traditions of the Covenanters* tells how Cannon never really took his faith seriously, which disturbed Fraser considerably. While Fraser was trying to concentrate on Semple's preaching, Cannon would be making signs to him and using other means to distract him from the message. It would seem that Cannon's was a mere outward religion and he never knew the transforming power of the gospel in his heart; whereas John Fraser became an enthusiastic follower of his Lord, with a deep heart commitment to his Saviour.

Cannon was a follower of the Covenanting cause at the beginning and joined the Glenkens Uprising which came to such a sorry end at Rullion Green in the Pentlands. Sir James Turner in his Memoirs even records how Mondrogat stayed behind briefly at Lanark with some men to destroy the ferry-boat and hold up Dalziel's advance. But after he was arrested, to save his own skin, he capitulated and became a notorious informer against the brethren. He was renowned for his lewdness, blasphemy, cursing and swearing, and open cruelty. In the service of his new masters Cannon was zealous in his persecution of those who stood firm for the Covenanting cause. One such was his old companion John Fraser. Fraser was alleged to have been a close friend of the field preacher Richard Cameron, and the soldiers were keen to track down any who were seen as associates of Cameron, who was killed at Ayrsmoss in 1680.

John Fraser found it necessary to be always on his guard, and at times to withdraw from his home when he sensed danger. The laird of Muirdrogat regularly sent the soldiers to his house when he thought there was a likelihood that he was at home. On every occasion when any work was to be done on the farm which required Fraser's superintendence, the dragoons were sure to make their appearance. At one time when he was directing the operations of his servants, who were employed in some work that needed his oversight, a company of horsemen were seen approaching. Fraser saw it was too late to take to the fields, and sought instead a place of concealment in his house. He ran into a small closet and hid himself under the bed clothes, fearing that it was unlikely that he would escape capture. But the quick action of one of his domestic servants saved the day. She heaped some wet turfs on the fire which, as was common in those days, stood in the middle of the kitchen. The house was quickly filled with dense blue smoke. The soldiers entered the house, but struggled to see anything in the murk. Most of them didn't tarry long in the house, but one did come upon Fraser in the small ante-chamber. Suspecting he'd found the one they sought, he asked him to sing a bawdy song. This Fraser refused to do, instead singing some lines of an old hymn, 'For all the babes in Bethlehem town King Herod sent and slew'. This confirmed to the dragoon that he had found his man. But whether through his conscience being pricked, or Fraser's earnest prayer for the Lord's protection being answered, or both of these, the soldier left the house and joined his fellow soldiers searching all the outbuildings without saying a word. Fraser watched for his opportunity, then slipped out into the hills with his shepherd's plaid across his shoulders and his dog trudging by his side.

Another time he experienced a similar deliverance. The troopers arrived suddenly at the house before anyone had noticed them approaching. They quickly stationed themselves at all the doors and windows to prevent anyone escaping. John Fraser was inside and, seeing that the front door was guarded, he ran to a small window at the back of the house. But as he was squeezing out through it he was confronted by the soldier who was posted there on his own. "So ho! You are there, friend, are you? – the very man, on the word of an honourable cavalier," muttered the dragoon, as John dragged himself from the aperture and stood before the burly sentinel. "I am in your power," said the worthy man. "Yes," replied the trooper, "but I feel, somehow or other, as if I were not inclined at present to use that power; nobody is witness to our encounter – run to that thicket and hide yourself; do not flee to the hill, for your flight might perchance be seen; and though you were as light of foot as a roe, our fleet horses will outrun you." The thicket to which the kindly soldier pointed was a dense willow bush which grew on the edge of the burn. And there he hid until the soldiers withdrew, thankful that the God to whom he had cried had again disposed one of his enemies to show him favour at a moment when he had despaired of escape.

These incidents strengthened his faith in God and trust in his mercy and protection. Another time he had retired for safety to the barn, to sleep among the straw with some wool blankets to keep him warm, expecting that the soldiers if they came would search the main house first and thus give him a chance of escape. In the middle of the night the dragoons arrived, the snow on the ground muffling the sound of the horses' hooves. After posting three troopers around the house to look out for anyone escaping, they went first to the stable to seek shelter for their horses and called up to the stable boy in the loft above, whom they had always managed to rouse easily before. However he was sound asleep and when there was no answer they suspected some Covenanters were hiding there. They called in the other three troopers to assist them and in the commotion John Fraser awoke in the adjacent barn and, slipping out, ran through the snow for three miles to the home of a friend. Meanwhile the soldiers found no one in the stable but the stable boy and proceeded to the main house where they found no sign of John either. When they entered the barn they found his bed still warm and vented their fury at their quarry eluding them again by seizing many items in the house and destroying what they could not carry away.

At another critical moment John Fraser owed his deliverance to the following. In former times the farm houses were the principal places of refuge for the wandering poor, who sought from the hospitable inhabitants a morsel of bread and a night's lodging. They were rarely turned away, especially in the moorland districts where there were less places for them to go. Because of the number of such vagrants there was generally a corner of the barn furnished with soft hay and warm blankets where they could spend the night after family worship and a good supper. In some houses it was a small room in the main house in which stood what was called 'the poor man's bed' and which was seldom without an occupant. One night when John Fraser thought he was safe, a company of soldiers rode up to the door in the dead of night, with the plan of surprising the family at an unusual hour, and quickly surrounded the house. Fraser saw little hope of escape this time. But his wife, nearly at her wits end with anxiety, suddenly pointed to the poor man's bed and urged him to run to it without delay. He did so, and she covered him hastily with tattered clothes and an old rug. The dragoons entered and did their usual search without finding him. They knew the house well, and they knew the poor man's bed and the kind of people who occupied it. They saw someone in the bed but turned away without disturbing the poor man in his resting place, never realising that he was the one they sought. So once again he evaded capture.

Simpson records that he was friendly with John Clerk of Glenhead a little further down the valley. Both had been friendly with Richard Cameron, which meant they were eagerly sought by the soldiers. Moreover Clerk in his wanderings had attached himself for a time to Rev Alexander Peden, also known as Prophet Peden, one of the leading figures in the Covenanter movement in Scotland. Fraser and Clerk often took refuge in a cave on Strahanna farm. On one occasion when they were hiding there an informer alerted Grierson of Lag in Carsphairn concerning their hiding place. When they saw the troopers approaching they fled for their lives. As they crossed a field where a man was mowing, they realised they were out of sight of their pursuers and hid themselves beneath the long rows of newly cut grass. The horsemen passed by, unaware of their hiding place, and they evaded capture. However they realised that it would be dangerous to remain in the neighbourhood and sought refuge in the home of Fraser's brother, Luke Fraser, at Glenmead (Glenmaid) in the hills near the village of Ae.

While at Glenmead Fraser and his brother and Clerk, along with four others, were captured by a party of dragoons and taken up to Edinburgh. When they arrived there it was found that all the jails were full and they were housed in the garret rooms of a neighbouring house as a temporary prison. It would seem that at least one of their wives had followed them to Edinburgh and was able to pass food to them through their warders. She came up with a clever plan. On assessing the height of the building she bought a rope and, coiling it neatly, placed it in some curds which she formed into the shape of a large cheese. When it had hardened sufficiently she took it to the house and it was passed to the prisoners. When they discovered the rope they made plans for their escape. Their rooms were close to the roof and they made a hole wide enough for them to squeeze through. In the middle of the night, when all was silent in the street below, they lowered the rope and began their descent. The last to descend was the husband of the cheesemaker who was heavier than the others and had insisted the others go first in case the rope would not bear his weight. Unfortunately when he was about halfway down the rope broke. The others below were ready to catch him and partially broke his fall. However he was seriously injured and could not walk. They quickly escaped from the city carrying their injured friend, leaving him at a cottage not far outside it. Later that day he was discovered there and carried back to prison. Shortly after he was condemned by the Privy Council and executed. However his companions managed to escape back to the south-west.

After this John Fraser was almost a constant exile from his house, staying up on the moors or in other hiding places with others seeking refuge from capture. Many times the soldiers came and found no sign of him. His heart however was with his home and his loved ones, and he returned when he could. One evening he came to his house about midnight and enjoyed some happy hours with his family. At dawn he was about to return to his hiding place, but his wife Marion prevailed upon him to linger with them a little longer. They spent a peaceful day together at the Upper Holm of Dalquhairn and John planned to slip away at dusk. But it was not to be. The troopers suddenly descended upon them as the family were comfortably seated round the dinner table. The troopers entered the house and seized him where he sat. They bound him firmly with ropes, tying his arms behind his back, then carried him to the stable and cast him into one of the stalls, where they left him and locked the door behind them. Having thus secured their prey, they proceeded to the dwelling-house, where they entertained themselves with a plentiful meal at their captive's expense. They were full of delight at having finally caught their man and in celebration turned to consume all the ale and liquor they could find in the house.

In the solitude of the stable John prayed to the God of his life who had hitherto delivered him, and whom he trusted could deliver him still. He wriggled across the floor into the darkest corner of the stable and managed to raise himself to his feet and squeeze himself into that corner. At length the soldiers finished partying and entered the stable reeling and staggering among the horses, too drunk to really know what they were doing. Having led their steeds into the open air, with some difficulty they mounted and then rode off in a noisy and disorderly manner, leaving behind the prize which was the whole reason for their celebrations. Marion ran to the stable and found her husband standing safe in the corner. She cut him free. They knew however that when the drunken soldiers discovered their mistake their fury would know no bounds; and Marion decided to join her husband in flight to a safe hiding place, leaving the children in the care of a servant. They hadn't long departed when the dragoons returned. When they found Fraser and his wife gone they proceeded to work all the mischief they could upon their home before heading off into the night. In the following days John and Marion returned briefly from the hills when they could to comfort their children, but they were distressing days for the family. Thankfully it wasn't long before the end of the times of persecution, after which they were then able to return to their family and pick up the pieces of family life again at their home in the heart of the hills. They had survived their times of trial and persecution. They were an example of a peaceful and pious couple who went through dark days, facing terrors in the night, but emerged at the end giving praise to the God of their salvation.

Fig. 14 (above): View towards 'The Lorg', with Whig's Hole on upper slope on right.
Fig. 15 (below): The isolated shepherd's cottage of 'The Lorg'.

8
THE LORG AND WHIG'S HOLE

Two kilometres north-east of the Holm of Dalquhairn is the isolated shepherd's cottage of 'The Lorg', now no longer with a permanent resident (Figs. 14 and 15). The area around it in the heart of the hills would seem to have been a home and refuge for many with strong sympathy for the Covenanting cause. Mark Jardine has provided convincing evidence for the Lorg having been occupied by the McMichael family for at least a hundred years prior to Covenanting times. It used to go by the name of Lorgfoot, as depicted on Roy's map of the 1750s. For many years Lorgfoot, the residence of Daniel McMichael, who was shot dead at Dalveen, was falsely identified with Blairfoot in Morton parish. He is listed as living at Lurg-foot in Dumfriesshire in the Fugitives' List of 1684. However it would seem that Daniel was very much a Glenkens man. Jardine, in his online blog, records a 1682 instrument of sasine witnessed by James McMichael in Lorgfoot, James McMichael, his son and heir, and John Amilliganc in Holm of Dalquhairn. Simpson claims that James and Daniel were born at Dalzean in Penpont parish, which is only a few miles south-east of Lorgfoot on the Scar Water. James junior, who died at Auchencloy in December 1684, is recorded in the 1684 Fugitives' List as residing at that time in Dalry. The list of 'disorderly persons' not attending church compiled by Carsphairn curate Peter Peirson in 1683 mentions James McMichael and his family living at the Holm of Dalquhairn, and the 1684 list has James McMichael and his daughter Elizabeth living at that place. As a number of families are recorded as living there and there is no mention of Lorgfoot, it is likely that a number of dwellings including Lorgfoot were included under the Holm of Dalquhairn. However to complicate matters a further James McMichael senior and his family is recorded as living at Glen (grid reference NX 636964), three or four miles down the valley from Lorgfoot. The second of the two lists specifically mentions this latter individual's son James. The list also names Roger McMichael in nearby Strahanna. In August 1684 James senior of Glen was accused in the Privy Council records of conversing with rebel David McKill in Dalshangan. Further, the Fugitives' List also names a Robert McMichael in Craiglour, near Carroch in Dalry parish and a Rebecca McMichael in Blackcraig in Dalry parish; so clearly a number of the McMichael family were supportive of the Covenanting cause and living in this part of the Glenkens.

In the previous chapter I recounted the tale of John Fraser of the Upper Holm of Dalquhairn, just over a mile down the valley from the Lorg. Simpson records that Fraser was friendly with John Clerk of Glenhead a little further to the south, just up the side valley from Glen. The Fugitives' Roll locates John Clerk at Polskeoch, a mile and a half east of the Lorg. And around the same time rebel John Clerk is said to hail from Marbrack – which may have been the family home as Peirson's list records James Clerk and his family as living there. Peirson also records other Clerk families living at Moorbrock, Strahanna and Holm of Dalquhairn, so there must have been an extended family network in the vicinity. Although it is possible that the authorities were seeking a number of Covenanters by the name of John Clerk, it is perhaps more likely that this shows how fugitives moved around to avoid capture.

It is probable that Daniel McMichael was involved in the Enterkin attack on 29th July 1684 when some Covenanter prisoners were freed. Certainly the Privy Council records mention that he was seen in the vicinity in the company of William Herries, who was certainly involved in the attack, armed with swords and guns. And in the preceding months a number of people testified that he had dropped in on their homes in Penpont parish with John Clerk of Polskeoch and other rebels, usually under the cloak of night, seeking food and drink. He had a price on his head, dead or alive, of 1000 merks, for subscribing to the Sanquhar Declaration and for being present when the Declaration was proclaimed on 22nd June 1680.

Daniel was captured in Morton parish on 30th January 1685. He had been hiding with some other Covenanters in a summer shieling in that parish when they were surprised by a party of soldiers. The rest managed to escape, but Daniel at that time was unwell and he didn't have the energy to make good his escape. The next day he was marched north to Dalveen in Durisdeer parish, near to the place where the Enterkin attack had taken place, where he was shot dead. He was allowed to pray before he died, and sang the metrical psalm 42, which begins, 'Like as the hart for water-brooks in thirst doth pant and bray, so pants my longing soul, O God, that come to thee I may. My soul for God, the living God, doth thirst: when shall I near unto thy countenance approach, and in God's sight appear?' He then read from John Ch.16, which begins, 'These things have I spoken unto you that ye should not be offended. They shall put you out of the synagogues: yea, the time cometh, that whosoever killeth you will think that he doeth God service.' A blindfold was then put around his head and he prayed, 'Lord, thou brought Daniel through many straits, and hast brought me, thy servant, hither to witness for thee and thy cause; into thy hands I commit my spirit, and I hope to praise thee through all eternity.' Four of the soldiers then shot him dead. It is recorded that some of the soldiers were deeply affected by the manner in which he embraced his death.

Shortly before you reach the Lorg as you come up the valley from the south if you look across the Water of Ken and high up on the slopes of Altry Hill you might be able to make out a feature called the Whig's Hole (grid reference NS 670001) where Covenanters used to meet for worship. It is hard to make out from below, but if you climb up the slope you come upon a shallow cleft in the side of the hill which could perhaps hold forty people (Fig. 16). We held

Fig. 16: Whig's Hole, in slight cleft near top of hill.

a conventicle on the valley bottom in 2005, singing 'The Lord's my Shepherd' amongst sheep and lambs beside the tumbling burn, after which the fittest members of our gathering climbed up to the place and sang a psalm for those in the valley below.

Simpson in his book on the Covenanters has this to say, though he refers to it as 'Whig Holes' rather than Whig's Hole. He writes, 'Towards the source of the Ken there is a hollow place called the 'Whig Holes', a secret retreat on the side of the mountain of Altry, where, in the covenanting times, the assemblies of God's people frequently convened for divine worship. The place is far up on the breast of the hill, and affords a seclusion so perfect that no company of troopers travelling in the plains below could even see the place, far less discern who were in it. A rising ground, like a green wall, stands in front, concealing immediately behind it a deep basin, while the mountain shoots aloft to a great height, and beneath descends precipitously to the brink of the Ken. It is said that when a conventicle happened to be held here, a warder was placed on each side of the basin, where an extensive view is obtained in the direction of Carsphairn on the one hand, and on the other, a full prospect towards the source of the river. The line along this sweetly secluded stream was the route of the military between Sanquhar and Carsphairn, and hence more than ordinary precautions were required on the part of the covenanters when at any time they happened to meet on the hill. The 'Whig Holes' was selected not only as a place of security, but also as a meeting place for the people of the upper parts of Nithsdale and the higher parts of Galloway; and many a time has the hallowed sound of praise ascended from the steep slopes of the lofty Altry. The shepherds in the vicinity of this place are proud to point out to the passing traveller the spot where the people congregated, at the risk of their lives, to maintain the standard of the Gospel among the lonely mountains.'

Those who are even more energetic and would like a full day in the hills might take a walk up to Allan's Cairn on the Southern Upland Way at grid reference NS 698008. George Allan and Margaret Gracie were shot on the Fawns of Altry, an area of open moorland one kilometre east of the Whig's Hole. The monument to their memory was placed on the nearby junction of three parish boundaries.

9
MARSCALLOCH

Rev Robert Simpson, who published the book *Traditions of the Covenanters* in 1841, wrote a later article on 'The Martyrs of Glendeugh' which was published in The Original Secession Magazine (1852-54) Vol.1, p.508-15. In it he recounts the story of William Smith and Mary McClymont. He wrote that William Smith was the son of Robert Smith of Deughside, a small pastoral farm nearby, later renamed Bridge of Deugh. The ruins of this house are now under the waters of Kendoon Loch. His is the only published account of the deaths of these two individuals. However the Register of the Privy Council in 1668 lists William Smith of Bridge of Deugh among the rebels for which it calls for the arrest.

According to Simpson, Robert and William Smith were at the battle of Bothwell Bridge in 1679 where the Covenanters were routed and Robert was wounded. They managed home to Deughside but Robert died soon after. His son William knew he was no longer safe at home and resolved to leave his younger brother and sisters at home and seek refuge amongst the hills and crags, as did so many of the persecuted brethren. However even before he had left home he was spied by one of his neighbours, Robert Cannon of Muirdrochwood (Mondrogat), a former Covenanter who had turned into a bitter enemy of the Covenanters and who set a passing band of Claverhouse's dragoons upon him. Smith had a lucky escape from them, hiding under a small turf-covered bridge nearby. He had his faithful dog with him and feared it would give him away, but mercifully it fled over the hill and did not return until the coast was clear.

The frustrated soldiers returned to the garrison at Carsphairn, on the way arresting a young woman they ran into whom they suspected must have seen Smith. But she had not, and despite applying the thumbscrews to her to try and get a confession they could get nothing from her. She was Mary McClymont, who will crop up later in our story. Smith returned to his house during the night; but the following evening Cannon returned with a party of dragoons, determined to get his reward for Smith's capture. Thankfully the barking of his dog warned him in time and he fled out the back of the house and found shelter in the hills. He hid with four other men for a time in a small cave at Craigdow in Kirkoswald parish until it became unsafe and they scattered, Smith finding a new hiding place in a deep linn on the farm of Camreggan near Dailly. He was led to that hiding place by a young woman whom he met nearby who was supplying food to two other men who were already hiding there. This young woman was Mary McClymont, daughter of Gavin McClymont of Dalmellington – who had gone to stay with

Fig. 17: House of Glenmuick, just over Ayrshire border on Dalmellington road.

116

her uncle at Camreggan. Her father had suffered grievously for the cause and Mary had thrown her youthful energies into supporting it in whatever way she could.

After a time their hiding place was discovered by a spy and they had to flee for their lives. Mary McClymont fled to her relatives at Glenmuick south of Dalmellington, and by coincidence William Smith found a new hiding place at Wolf Craig among the rocky cliffs which bound the Muick to the north of Glenmuick. Glenmuick is the first house one comes to after passing north into Ayrshire (Fig. 17). There one of the Glenmuick shepherds caught sight of Smith and mentioned this in Mary's hearing. The next evening she hid near the place where he had been seen and saw her friend returning to his hiding place. The following day she took some food to his secret lair, though he wasn't there at the time; and for a number of days she left food there for him while he was absent. On the fourth day troops were in the area and she stayed at home. In the evening they came to the house and roughly questioned her. She dashed out the door and along a narrow path followed by the drunken troopers, one of whom thrust at her with his sword and fell over a precipice to his death. The following morning Mary found the weapon and conveyed it to her friend. They were reunited and not long afterwards during a period when the persecution was less intense they were married at a conventicle held in a glen near the farmhouse of Bowmoor on the Water of Deugh. However Smith still returned to Wolf Craig each night and Mary to Glenmuick. Both of them were actively sought by the troops as ringleaders of the rebellion. To help protect them the local shepherds constructed a secret chamber within a peat stack that they built against the gable end of Glenmuick, with access from the interior of the house. For many months they used this hideout when danger threatened and were able to know some of the privacy that any husband and wife should know.

During a brief lull in the persecution conventicles were again held and the people sought to encourage one another in the faith. Cannon of Muirdrochwood heard of a conventicle taking place on the boundary between Dundeugh and Marscalloch in 1684, alerted his friend McMillan, who was also a persecutor of the Covenanters, and they rushed to call out the soldiers of the garrison at Carsphairn. Within an hour they had surrounded the conventicle. Smith and his wife with a few other trusty friends took their stand near the minister, Smith wielding the sword Mary had given him. Most of the people fled, a number on both sides being injured as they rushed to escape. McMillan approached Smith and entered into combat with him. For a time neither had the upper hand, until McMillan dashed his military cap in his opponent's face and ran him through the heart. Mary then seized Smith's sword and struggled with his murderer, who quickly overcame her and dispatched her also. It was said that from the sword wound in her breast flowed forth a mixture of milk and blood, so by this stage she must have been nursing an infant who was left motherless.

It is said that McMillan was then filled with remorse and swore never to use his sword against the Covenanters again. He returned that night with two or three of the more trusty soldiers to bury the two bodies in the moss near where they fell before they were further abused by man or beast. He took an oath with his assistants never to reveal where they were buried or that they had done this deed. In a later unpublished account deposited in Stranraer Museum Simpson mentions that around 1830 local people cutting peat on Marscalloch Moss came upon two well preserved human bodies which they believed to be those of the two martyrs, William and Mary. We don't know where exactly that place was, but no doubt they covered their bodies up again and left them to rest in peace. Their bodies may rest in the peat, but their souls will have passed on to a higher sphere where they see their Saviour face to face. They paid the ultimate price for their commitment to the cause of Christ. We held a conventicle at Marscalloch in 2009 in their memory.

10
CARSPHAIRN

Carsphairn village is a small hamlet situated in the heart of the hills on Galloway's northern fringe. Carsphairn parish only came into existence by an Act of the Scottish Parliament in 1645 when it was created out of the northern parts of Kells and Dalry parishes. Prior to that the people of the surrounding area had got together and built a church at their own expense in 1635-6 and so there was an energy and commitment from the people to support and build their new church community. When Charles I tried to introduce the Episcopalian form of worship in 1638 no doubt there was strong local support for the National Covenant which was signed all around Scotland that year.

When the new parish was set up an inspiring, charismatic figure entered the scene. John Semple had gone over to Ulster to support the Scottish ministers who were seeking to establish Presbyterian worship amongst the Scots emigrants of the Ulster Plantation. And he had made a bit of a name for himself as a field preacher in the times of revival that spread through the community there. Semple came back to Kirkcudbright and offered himself for the ministry of the Church of Scotland. He was of fairly humble background and didn't have the knowledge of the Latin language that was normally required of ministers. But the Presbytery of Kirkcudbright recognised his God-given gifts for communicating the Christian message and thought what better person could there be to build up and strengthen the new church amongst the wild hill folk of Carsphairn. Their choice was an inspired one and John Semple threw himself into the challenge of building up Christ's church in this new parish and discipling the local folk. He was appointed as the first parish minister in 1646. He quickly made a name for himself throughout the area and became one of the leaders of the covenanting movement. His communion seasons gathered people from far and wide; and at these communion gatherings where many other local ministers would also preach in Carsphairn, Semple was above all the man people came to hear. He was renowned as an inspiring spiritual figure and a man of the people. He inspired a religion of the heart, building a deep commitment of the local people to their Lord and Saviour, Jesus Christ.

I mentioned in Chapter 1 that Semple was a well-known national figure among the Covenanters and had the boldness to oppose Oliver Cromwell to his face. For this he suffered six months' imprisonment. Inevitably Semple's presence put Carsphairn at the heart of the covenanting struggle when times of persecution came in 1662 under Charles II, and Semple, like all the other local ministers, was evicted from his pulpit. He was allowed to return to his own pulpit in 1672 on condition that he did not hold conventicles. More extreme covenanters considered this a compromise, but Semple considered his first calling was to be there as shepherd of his sheep in Carsphairn parish in the midst of their times of trial and persecution. He was still unapologetically his own person and at times ran into conflict with the authorities. He died in Carsphairn in 1677 at the age of 75 and was buried in the churchyard, though no legible stone records his resting place.

The government authorities recognised that they had to come down heavily on Carsphairn as a hotbed of covenanting sympathies if they were going to establish the new church order. One brave curate (though he called himself Carsphairn's rector), bachelor Peter Peirson, volunteered to come and take on that challenge. He became friendly with the arch persecutor of the covenanters, Robert Grierson of Lag, who would often base himself with a military garrison at the nearby farm of Garryhorn. There was also for a time another military garrison stationed in Carsphairn village itself. Not surprisingly very few people attended Peirson's services in the church and in 1683 and 1684 Peirson produced

Fig. 18: Carsphairn Church and churchyard.

lists of nearly all his parishioners, naming them 'disorderly' for not attending church. He was directly responsible for the arrest and subsequent death or transportation of 21 local people. In December 1684 things came to a head when a small delegation went to the manse to ask him to desist from his persecution of his own parishioners; and in an ensuing scuffle he was shot dead. James McMichael was judged the guilty party and he had a reputation for being a bit of a hothead. He claimed the shooting was an accident, though he was to lose his own life a few days later on Auchencloy Moor near New Galloway. (For more information on McMichael, see the chapters on Auchencloy Moor, on Dalry churchyard and on The Lorg and Whig's Hole.)

ROGER DUNN
Carsphairn churchyard has inscriptions commemorating two

covenanters (Fig. 18). Just to the left of the entrance gates there is a stone which reads:

"Erected in memory of Rodger Dunn, who was born in Benwhat, in the parish of Dalmellington, 1659. He suffered much from persecution for the cause of Christ, and was killed on the night of Carsphairn Fair, June 1689, on the farm of Brockloch."

Simpson in his 1841 book *Traditions of the Covenanters* has the following:

'A few notices may here be given of Roger Dun, a noted Covenanter, who lived in the higher parts of Ayrshire... Roger Dun was born in 1659. His father, James Dun, a worthy man, was farmer of Benwhat in the parish of Dalmellington, and was, with others, exposed to no small trouble in those trying times. Roger, when he grew up, and was able to judge for himself, resolved to share the fortunes of the Covenanters. It was soon known that Roger Dun had allied himself to the obnoxious party, and therefore his ruin was determined on. A conventicle had been held at Craignew in Carsphairn [possibly at Craignaw south of Loch Trool and actually in Monigaff parish] and Roger, with two of his brothers, attended the meeting. The report of this circumstance soon spread, and the dragoons were sent to apprehend all they could find returning from this place. They met the three brothers on the way home – Andrew and Allan were made prisoners, and carried back to Carsphairn; but what befell them is not known, for they were never more heard of. [Other writers suggest that the names of his two brothers were actually James and Robert Dunn, whom we meet later in the story.] Roger, however, by a sudden and unexpected spring, eluded the grasp of the soldier who attempted to seize him; and bounding away, fled to a soft marshy place into which the horsemen dared not venture, and made his escape. After this, Dun sought a retreat in Dunaskin Glen, a place about two miles from Benwhat. One morning, as he was returning home from his hiding place, he encountered, unexpectedly, a party of dragoons who were sent out in search of him. He was so near them that to attempt flight was in vain. In order, therefore, to avoid suspicion, he appeared to be as much at ease as possible, and walking forward with an undaunted mien, he determined to accost the soldiers in a style that would tend to direct their attention away from himself. "I think I can guess your errand, gentlemen," addressing the troopers in a familiar manner; "I am thinking you are in search of Roger Dun, who is supposed to be in concealment somewhere in this quarter?" "It is even so," replied the commander of the party; "he is the very person we are in quest of." "Well," said Roger, "though I hate the name of an informer, yet I think I could direct you to a place in which he is sometimes to be found. See you yon shepherd's hut afar in the waste; bear down directly upon it, and see what you can find." "You are an honest fellow, I opine," answered the leader; "and we will follow your advice." The party then proceeded onward at full speed, and Roger, with all expedition, betook himself to his hiding place in the glen, which is said to have been beneath the projecting bank of a mountain streamlet. In this seclusion, where the hallowed voice of prayer often mingled with the soft murmuring of a silvery brook, he found a place of safety from man, and of communion with his God.

On another occasion, when Roger had crept from his concealment, and found his way unperceived to his father's house, he was surprised by the hasty arrival of a company of troopers before the door. He attempted to escape through an aperture in the gable of the house, but it being partly closed up with rubbish, he was hindered from making his way with the speed that was desirable. When the soldiers entered, Roger was gone, but they found a youth of sixteen years of age [most probably his younger brother Quintin, who was banished to the Jamaican plantations in the summer of 1685], who had not time to follow his friend; him they seized, and how he was disposed of none could tell, for he was never again seen in the country. Dun made his way through a morass, leaving his pursuers behind him, and got with all safety into his retreat in Glenasken [Dunaskin Glen].

From the incessant harassment to which he was subjected, Roger Dun found it necessary to leave the district, and to retire to the lower parts of Galloway. When he was in the neighbourhood of Minigaff, residing in the house of a friend who was favourable to the cause in which he suffered hardship, he nearly lost his life by the hand of the enemy. The soldiers having made an attack on the house in which he was lodged, two of its inmates were killed defending themselves; and Dun, after an ineffectual resistance, fled, and plunging into the waters of a neighbouring loch, swam under water to a shallow place in the middle, where grew several shrubs and willows, at the side of which he emerged, while the soldiers shot into the lake at random. Owing to this immersion in the cold waters, he got a severe fever, which threatened to terminate his life, but from which he ultimately recovered.'

Thomson in his 1875 book *Martyr Graves* gives a slightly different version:

'The tradition is that it was on a Sabbath morning, and when they were engaged in prayer and in reading the Scriptures, that the dragoons surprised the six martyrs; the seventh, a Dun, the brother of the two Duns that were shot [James and Robert] managed to escape from the house, and was closely pursued by two of the soldiers. Seeing no other way of safety, he made for Loch Trool. For a moment a little hill concealed him from view of his pursuers as he ran into the water. Once in the loch he got in among the reeds, where, although his head was above water, he was entirely out of sight. The soldiers fired at random, but no shot came near him. How long he remained standing up to his neck in water is not recorded, but he remained so long – and the time was the month of January – that he shivered with cold and caught fever. When he came out he took refuge in a house close to the loch. Here the inmates sent him to bed while his clothes were drying. The fever soon appeared, and raged with great violence until his life was despaired of. A young woman in the house carefully nursed him during his illness. At last he recovered, and the story pleasantly ends by saying that after a time Dun married his nurse.'

This almost certainly looks like an account of the incident at Caldons near Loch Trool in January 1685 in which Captain Alexander Urquhart of his Majesties Regiment of Foot Guards and a number of Covenanters were killed. It would seem that most of the Covenanters killed at Caldons had taken to hiding deep in the hills along the Carrick/Galloway border in the winter of 1684 to 85; and that the Dunn brothers had abandoned the area around their homes near Dalmellington to seek refuge in the remote hill houses at Starr just south of Loch Doon. At some point, probably not long before the attack, they had moved further south into Galloway.

When Colonel James Douglas arrived in Galloway with 200 soldiers in January 1685 he planted three new garrisons at Machermore Castle, Earlstoun Castle and at Waterhead in Carsphairn parish. The latter was not too far from Starr and was the home of McAdam of Waterhead. This would have put more pressure on the Dunn family as Roger's sister was married to the covenanter Gilbert McAdam, Waterhead's son. Though the writers on the Covenanters give the impression that it was an innocent gathering of covenanters for worship that was attacked by Colonel Douglas and his troops, it could be that the Covenanters set out to attack the troops, whom they saw as a serious threat; and it was in this engagement that Captain Urquhart was killed.

Roger lived until after the Revolution of 1688, and was at last killed at Brockloch in Carsphairn parish after the end of the troubles by an individual who mistook him for another person whom he intended to murder; so that the worthy man, who had so often escaped the sword of the public persecutor, fell by the hand of a private assassin. It is possible that he was living at Garryhorn at that time. Most probably it was his son Robert who died at Garryhorn in 1738 and who is also named on his gravestone. Robert was living at Garryhorn in 1736. There is a record of another Robert Dunn who was a Carsphairn Church elder living at Woodhead in 1736, so it is likely that another branch of the Dunn family was living at Woodhead (which is near Brockloch) in 1689 – hence the case of mistaken identity.

GILBERT MCADAM OF WATERHEAD

The other Covenanter commemorated in Carsphairn churchyard is Gilbert McAdam. During the reign of King Charles II, the McAdams were ardent covenanters. Gilbert McAdam, younger, of Waterhead, early made a name for himself as a bit of a hothead. He was hauled before the Privy Council in Edinburgh in 1671 accused of being the ringleader in beating up the former curate of Carsphairn David McQuherne when he came back to claim unpaid stipend. He was fined for this incident. Though there was clearly another side to this incident; for at the same time a case was brought by Gilbert McOrnock of Carnavel and John McMillan of Drumness that the same day David McQuherne along with others had come to the house of David McOrnock with swords and pistols, broken down his door, seized the keys to the chest in which he kept public money as the collector of the King's taxes and beaten up his wife. That case was not proven.

Gilbert fought at the Battle of Bothwell Bridge in 1679. He was arrested for non-attendance at his parish church in Carsphairn in 1682 and taken to Dumfries, from where he was released on bail of £400 scots provided by his father-in-law James Dunn of Benwhat and returned to Waterhead. He did not turn up for his trial and so the money was forfeited. Soon after he was apprehended and taken to Glasgow where, on refusing to take the test where he was asked to affirm that the king was the head of the church, he was banished to the plantations in America. When sailing away to the Carolinas in 1684 his father gave him £20, and with this sum he succeeded after his arrival in purchasing his freedom and returning home early the next year.

Not long afterwards, he attended a prayer meeting at a cottage in Kirkmichael in south Ayrshire in June 1685. Meetings such as this, along with those held in the open air, were illegal, and the cottage was surrounded by a party of armed soldiers, led by Sir Archibald Kennedy of Culzean and John Reid of Ballochmyle. While trying to escape out a window, Gilbert McAdam was shot and killed. He was buried in Kirkmichael churchyard where a stone reads, 'Here lies Gilbert McAdam who was shot in this parish by the Laird of Culzean and Balochmyl for his adherence to the Word of God and Scotland's Covenanted work of Reformation 1685.' There is also an inscription commemorating the event over the entrance to the McAdam burial place in Carsphairn graveyard, which lies at the east end of the church, though now hard to read. Despite the Kirkmichael stone, some believe that the body of Gilbert McAdam is interred at Carsphairn. His son James, was also a zealous Covenanter, and narrowly escaped being shot when his uncle, Roger Dunn, was killed.

MCRORY OF HALFMARK

Simpson records another covenanter martyr who lived just outside Carsphairn village – McRory of Halfmark - though his name is not preserved in historical documents of the time. Near the confluence of the Garryhorn and Halfmark Burns at grid reference NX 553927 there are the scant remains of a humble dwelling that was still lived in during the 1850s. But McRory is said to have lived there over 300 years ago. I will let Simpson in his book *Traditions of the Covenanters* take up the story:

'There lived in the parish of Carsphairn, at a place called Halfmark, in the vicinity of Garryhorn, Lagg's residence, a person of the name of McRory. This man was a Covenanter, and was in reality what he professed to be, a holy and upright character. He was a peaceable and unobtrusive man, and one who took great delight in reading the Scriptures and in prayer. It happened one Sabbath morning that this good man, having driven his cows to the fields to graze, sat down on the turf, and having taken the sacred volume from the corner of his plaid, began to peruse its blessed contents as an exercise suitable at all times, but more especially on the holy Sabbath. Lagg and his men, it would appear, were early abroad on the same morning, but for a very different purpose; their object was, not to worship God and to keep his Sabbath, but if possible, to suppress His worship, and to desecrate the hours of holy rest. They sallied out to seek their own pleasure on the Lord's day, and with a view to discover any small conventicle of worshippers in the moors, whom they might either capture or kill, as best suited their caprice. In their raid they came upon McRory devoutly studying the Word of God. The poor man had found his salvation in this Word, and now he was poring over it with a believing and a grateful heart, and enjoying more true satisfaction by far, in the possession of this treasure, than the men of the world can experience in all their riches and in all their fair and spacious inheritances. "The kingdom of heaven is like unto a treasure hid in a field; the which when a man hath found he hideth, and for joy thereof goeth and selleth all that he hath, and buyeth that field."

This lowly and heavenly-minded man, was, in spirit, holding converse with his God, when Lagg and his troopers came suddenly upon him. The good man was taken by surprise, but, by the grace of Him in whom he believed, he was ready for whatever event might befall. The ruthless persecutor asked, in a rough and imperious tone, what book he was reading? The pious man, looking up in his face, meekly replied: "It is the Bible." And who can tell how much He, who knew what was coming upon His faithful witness, had fortified his faithful heart for his hour of trial, by means of the consolations of that Gospel on which he was meditating at the very moment when his deadly foes presented themselves before him? The reading of the Bible was a sin not to be forgiven by Lagg, who, like the rest of his brotherhood employed in the same work of wickedness with himself, regarded it as a symptom of disloyalty that merited its appropriate punishment. When the honest man made the confession that it was the Word of God he was reading, Lagg instantly exclaimed, that his cows must forthwith find another herd, as his life, as a rebel, was now forfeited. McRory no sooner heard the sentence of death pronounced, than Lagg, without ceremony and without compunction, shot him dead on the spot. The summons was indeed hasty, and he was called, at a time and in a place he did not expect, to seal his testimony with his blood; but he was not unprepared to enter that rest in heaven, of which the Sabbath he had begun to keep holy on earth was a figure. His murderers left his bleeding body on the heath, and went onward, prepared to act a similar tragedy in the case of the next suspected person with whom they might happen to meet.'

This is all we know about McRory. Lag declared that his cattle must find another herd. Were there also a wife and young children left behind in their simple dwelling without a husband and father? And what was behind this cruel persecution and such a summary act of execution performed in cold blood? It would seem that McRory was a peace-loving and honest man seeking to live a godly Christian life. Robert Grierson of Lag on the other hand was notorious as one of the arch persecutors of the Covenanters. To hear Simpson again, writing of Lag and that other infamous persecutor Claverhouse:

> Lagg and Claverhouse were intimate friends, companions in wickedness, who delighted in debauchery and profanity, in pillaging and in bloodshed. Two characters more fitted for the work in which they were engaged could scarcely have been found. Galloway, Nithsdale, and Annandale, was the wide field over which they roamed, committing all kinds of wickedness, and perpetrating the most unrestrained acts of injustice, rapine, and cruelty.
>
> The district appointed them by the council was considered by them as their appropriate kingdom, within the limits of which they might do as they pleased, without the fear of being called to account, and without the least regard to the remonstrances of the peasantry.
>
> The names of these two men were terrible to the people, and their coming to any place was considered as a circumstance much more to be dreaded than the visitation of a pestilence; and men fled at the very report of them as from an invading army, and hid themselves in the mountain deserts and in the caves and holes of the earth. The distress of the people in certain localities is scarcely conceivable; and this distress was owing simply to the lawless ravages of these unprincipled Cavaliers, who rioted in mischief, and enriched themselves by the spoliation of their countrymen.

Lag lived in Dunscore parish, but his family held land in

other places also. In particular, he owned a swathe of land extending north from Garryhorn. So he hadn't just taken over the farm of Garryhorn but had a right to it and saw it as a very suitable base for himself when operating in this area – a place from which he could look down on the whole Carsphairn valley. McRory must have required some courage to continue living so near the wolf's lair. And it would suggest that, though he was a devout believer who identified with the covenanting cause, he was a man quietly minding his own business and had never felt a need to take to the hills for his safety. It is likely his martyrdom took place in 1685 in the Killing Times, soon after the killing of the Carsphairn curate. We held a conventicle at Halfmark in 2014.

So with the stories of these three individuals we get a snapshot of the troubled times the people of Carsphairn parish endured during the military occupation seeking to suppress the Covenanting movement.

Fig. 19 (above): View of Kells Church, looking down on Loch Ken.
Fig. 20 (below): Tombstone of Adam MacWhann in Kells
churchyard, set into new stone in 1832

11
KELLS CHURCHYARD

You will find Kells Church and its surrounding churchyard a little north of the Royal Burgh of New Galloway on the small side road to Glenlee. From the hillside above the church you can obtain a fine view looking down towards Loch Ken (Fig. 19).

One of the two Covenanter gravestones in Kells churchyard is for a local man by the name of Adam MacWhann (Fig. 20). For safety he spent much of his time hiding up in the high Galloway hills. On the 1:25,000 OS map you will find MacWhann's Stone marked by the side of the Curnelloch Burn nine miles west of New Galloway, at grid reference NX 491802 (Fig. 21). There Adam fashioned a secret hideout. Today this boulder is passed by a forest road, but in the 17th century it was far more remote and distant from any track. MacWhann had contracted a fever and become

Fig. 21: MacWhann's Stone near the Curnelloch Burn, NW of Clatteringshaws Loch.

extremely unwell, and this forced him to return to his home, which stood outside New Galloway, to seek refuge. Shortly after this, at the height of the Killing Times in 1685, Colonel James Douglas arrived at his home while he lay on his sick bed and barged into the house, pushing past his family who were caring for him. Finding the Covenanter lying there he put questions to him, but for some reason MacWhann was either unwilling or perhaps unable to answer them.

"Drag him to New Galloway," Douglas ordered. His soldiers took the sick man into the royal burgh where he was locked up for the night in the Town Hall jail. A couple of days later he was brought out and shot in the centre of the village. No trial had taken place. MacWhann's body was later carried to the churchyard and buried secretly by friends. The suggestion has been made that MacWhann had actually been involved in the skirmish at Caldons by Loch Trool a short while before, when a group of Covenanters had been surprised by a party of soldiers of His Majesty's Regiment of Foot Soldiers under the command of Col. Douglas. In the ensuing engagement six Covenanters had been killed, along with Captain Urquhart and two foot soldiers. Col. Douglas may indeed have been responding ruthlessly to the loss of his men.

In 1832 MacWhann's gravestone was set into a new stone erected in his memory with money raised from the inhabitants of New Galloway after a special sermon preached by the then minister James Maitland. It can be found to the south-west of the church. It is most likely that the original stone was moved at that time from the old graveyard around the pre-Reformation church nearby at Achie when that land was returned to agricultural use.

The second Covenanter stone is a tabletop one close to the eastern door of the church for the Gordons of Largmore up the Garroch Glen in Kells parish. After the Pentland Rising in 1666, which began in Dalry, persecution intensified and we first meet the Gordons of Largmore. John Gordon of Largmore was wounded at the Battle of Rullion Green when the Pentland Rising was quashed. He managed to make it home but his wounds were severe. Immediately after the Pentland Rising a regiment of 400 foot soldiers and 80 horsemen under Sir William Bannatyne was sent to Galloway and stationed mostly in the Glenkens. When Bannatyne heard that John Gordon was back home he at once ordered him to be brought to him dead or alive. The soldiers took a cart with them because they knew he wouldn't be fit to ride or walk. When they got to the house they told him he must go with them. Raising himself a little in his bed he answered that he now defied Sir William and all his persecutors, but he forgave them. Then he added that he would soon be in better company; and he lay down again and a few minutes later breathed his last. He was buried in Kells churchyard alongside his grandfather Roger Gordon of Largmore, who had died five years previously aged 72.

Roger's son, another Roger, had many close calls and survived the persecution. Roger Gordon junior was at the Battle of Bothwell Bridge, when the covenanters were routed, and fled south with some friends. Simpson in his 1841 book *Traditions of the Covenanters* tells how they were nearly caught at the home of a friend in Moniaive parish but hid in a secret cellar and avoided capture. Roger returned home, but he was a wanted man and his home was frequently visited by troopers, who rarely departed without perpetrating some act of mischief. So he was only able to snatch brief spells at home, usually under the cover of night. On one such occasion he had only just arrived when a company of troopers rode up to the door. He quickly put on the coarser and more tattered clothes of a farm servant and went to meet the visitors. He held the horses while they dismounted, then led the animals to the stables. While he assisted one of the dragoons to fodder the horses, the rest of the party got busy searching the house. In the darkness and confusion, under the pretence of taking a pitcher to fetch water for the horses, he took the opportunity to make himself scarce and headed as fast as he could for his favourite hiding place up in the hills.

On another occasion he was caught by the troops. As they entered the farmyard he was disappearing out the other end and they immediately apprehended him, suspecting he was the person they were seeking. They asked him if he was the Laird of Largmore and he replied that he was the Laird of Shinmount, the name of a hill on his estate. His answer threw them and, thinking they were mistaken, they let him go and proceeded to search the house; and he quickly slipped off to his place of concealment in the wilds. The advantage of not having photo-fit pictures in those days! These were only some of the close shaves he is recorded as having.

In his chapter on Roger Gordon of Largmore Simpson writes the following, referring to a time Roger escaped from the dragoons one night when they surprised him at Largmore: 'He then repaired, with all convenient speed, to his accustomed hiding-place in one of the lofty ranges of the Galloway mountains, called the *Mill* or *Meaul ae*. A place of greater solitude than this can scarcely be found, and a retreat which, in the night season, it was impossible for the troopers to find.'

His name for the mountain is a bit garbled, and to my mind this is clear evidence that he was attempting to write down stories that had been shared with him orally; but I'm sure he is referring to Meikle Millyea. Roger held the land of Clenrie as well so it would make sense that he might have built a refuge on the higher reaches of his land where he would have been unlikely to have been troubled by soldiers. In 2020, when climbing the mountain with my family, I came upon the ruins of a small building high up on the shoulder of the mountain (Fig. 22). I'm convinced it was Roger's secret hideout. I only noticed the ruin when I was almost upon it, and he would have likely camouflaged it with heather and have given it a turf roof, so that it would have been even less visible in those days. If it had been a summer shieling one might have expected to find some small outbuildings, and this building really seems to be too high up for it to be a shieling. If you are looking for a more challenging hike you can visit it at grid reference NX 52963 83404.

Fig. 22: Probable hideout of Roger Gordon high up on Meikle Millyea.

Roger was fortunate to survive the times of persecution, and lived on to know many happy days of peace and prosperity after the end of the troubles in 1689. Simpson says that he presented the parish of Kells with a large new bell in 1714, and a pair of communion cups also. A fine old bell hangs in Kells Church tower inscribed 'Ex Dono Gullielmi Gordon. Quirin de Visser Me Fecit Roterodami. Anno 1722' – (Donated by William Gordon. Quirin de Visser made me. Rotterdam 1722). So Simpson is clearly inaccurate in his information. Nor does Kells Church have communion cups presented to the church by Roger Gordon. But two cups were presented to Kells Church in 1721 – one by Andrew Ewart, who was minister from 1691 to 1739; and the other by William Newall of Barskeoch, who was a neighbour of Roger's up the Garroch Glen and also came from a family with covenanting sympathies.

I mentioned above that the bell was donated to the church

Fig. 23: Plaque set in the bell tower of Kells Church recording the gift of the bell to the church.

by William Gordon. Who was William Gordon? Intriguingly, there is a small stone plaque high up on the bell tower, which must originally have been set into the wall of a bell house which had housed the bell before the bell tower was added in 1822. It reads, 'WILLIAM GORDON SON TO JA GORDON J:OYE TO LARGMORE GIFTED THIS BELL 1722. SET UP 1724' (Fig. 23). I strongly suspect that James, who survived until 1730, well after the troubles, is the above 'Roger'. He was perhaps named James Roger, but often went by the name Roger to keep alive the name of his much-loved father. The fact that he is named Roger Gordon of

Largmore in the 1682 Kirkcudbrightshire Land Tax Roll supports this proposal. James had a son named William who became a merchant up in Glasgow and he most likely decided to present the bell to Kells Church in thankfulness to God for his father having survived the times of persecution.

Roger Gordon, the patriarch of the family who had died in 1662, had two sons when in his late fifties, John and James, who are buried alongside him in Kells churchyard. The above James is this son. His grandson John who died of his wounds was in fact slightly older than John and James, and was the son of Roger's son John from his earlier first marriage. James is designated as 'in Largmore' rather than 'of Largmore' in various documents, implying that he had not inherited his father's title to the land. (We find this, for example, in the account of the attack on Alexander McGhie's house in 1679 in which James was involved, referred to in Chapter 1 (p. 31). That title passed to the son (John) of the John who died of his wounds after Rullion Green. At first I was puzzled at the meaning of J:OYE TO in the inscription. However I then discovered that 'oye' is the old Scots word for 'grandchild'. It would seem that William is referring to his grandfather Roger, the patriarch of the family as 'Largmore'.

Fig. 24: Auchencloy Memorial

12
AUCHENCLOY MEMORIAL

The Auchencloy Memorial (Fig. 24) is more challenging to reach than most places referred to in this book. To reach it requires quite a long walk or cycle in along forestry tracks. It is accessed off the Raider's Road in the Galloway Forest Park. The Raider's Road is only open to vehicles between April and October. If driving in you will be able to drive no further than grid reference NX 617714, near to the ruins of Barney Water. There is a locked forestry barrier there. From there it is just over a kilometre's walk along the forestry road to NX 610703, where a track on the right starts, which takes one on the final kilometre or so to the memorial at NX 603708.

On 18th December 1684 eight Covenanters were run to ground on Auchencloy Moor by Graham of Claverhouse and a band of troopers. The events surrounding that last stand at Auchencloy have been covered in the chapter on Dalry churchyard. Two days before they had forced an entry into Kirkcudbright Tolbooth and released the Covenanters held there; but during that action a guard had been killed. One of their number was James McMichael, who had been accused of the killing of the curate of Carsphairn a week earlier (see chapter on Carsphairn). Tradition has it that they were fleeing for their lives towards a hideout on the Shaw of Orchars, the hill to the west, when the soldiers caught up with them. Escape from the mounted troopers was well-nigh impossible. But two of their number did manage to dash off as soon as they saw the approaching soldiers and made it safely away. The others made their last stand by the large boulder which lies alongside the later memorial. Claverhouse in his Memoirs records that the Covenanters fought for their lives with sword and pistol, and Claverhouse himself, who prided himself in his skill with the sword, engaged McMichael in mortal combat. Claverhouse was so hard pressed by McMichael's superior swordplay that he had to call upon the help of a sergeant of dragoons who rushed on McMichael from behind and cleaved his skull with one blow. On hearing Claverhouse call for help, McMichael is said to have exclaimed: 'You dare not abide the issue of a single combat; and had your helmet been like mine, a soft bonnet, your carcass had ere this found a bed upon the heath.'

The engagement at Auchencloy led to the death of four of the Covenanters – James McMichael, Robert Stewart, John Grierson and Robert Ferguson. The other two, William Hunter and Robert Smith, were bound and dragged off to Kirkcudbright, where they were garrotted to death and beheaded a few days later. Their graves can be seen in Kirkcudbright Cemetery. When the bodies of the four who had been killed were found by their friends, those of the three who came from Dalry parish were taken back there for burial (see chapter on Dalry Churchyard); while the body of Robert Ferguson, who came from Tynron parish, was buried at Auchencloy. Near the memorial you can still see there the stone placed over his grave (Fig. 25).

These men were active in standing up to the persecution, men unwilling to accept passively the injustice that was being meted out, men who displayed a reckless bravery – and men who had a strong sense of the justice of their cause, and were unwilling to compromise what they saw as central to their faith and beliefs. They were perhaps not so ready to turn the other cheek as their Lord would have been; but who can blame them for standing against the tyranny of the times? In the boldness of their faith they were an inspiration to others.

In August 1835 a conventicle was held there which was led by the minister of Girthon, Rev Robert Jeffrey. Auchencloy is just within Girthon parish. Its purpose was to raise funds for the building of a monument in memory of the Covenanters who died there. Newspaper reports of that day comment on how beforehand numerous bands of worshippers could be seen streaming towards the place from every point of the compass, as though gathering for a conventicle of old. We read in the Dumfries Times, 'The morning was wet and dreary, and had every appearance to be unfavourable for the occasion. The reverend gentleman entered the tent exactly at 12 o'clock, when, as by supernatural influence, the flowing mist in the hollows, and the lowering clouds disappeared in the glens and valleys, and fled to the mountain tops, and instantly the bright sun shone forth with all its splendour and glory, to welcome and favour the reverend speaker.' It was reckoned that at least 1500 people gathered for the service and that if the weather had been better probably double that number would have come. The tent referred to was a wooden tent covered with cloth set up as a temporary pulpit about three metres behind the grave. Details are preserved of all four psalms that were sung, and tunes for three of them. There was a reading from Daniel 3.8-19 and Robert Jeffrey took as his text verses 17 and 18, preaching a 50 minute sermon which was later published.

In 2006 I conducted a conventicle there beside the large boulder where the Covenanters had made their last stand. To access the site we had to make our way along tussocky firebreaks through the trees, and the midges were unrelenting in their attack on that day. The trees around the memorial have all now been cut down.

Fig. 25: Grave of Robert Ferguson beside Auchencloy Memorial, the stone being typical of those produced by Old Mortality.

Fig. 26 (above): Granite cobble marking Covenanter grave near the Palfern Burn; and Fig. 27 (below): Rev David Bartholomew alongside memorial stone dedicated in April 2013 near the Palfern Burn. The belt retrieved from the body can be seen in the photograph.

13
PALFERN BURN

This site of the burial of two unknown Covenanters lies west of Clatteringshaws Loch. To reach it one needs to take the forestry track roughly opposite the Red Deer Park south into the hills. When we held a conventicle there in 2013 the site of the burial was in the centre of a small unplanted oval area in the midst of forestry (Fig. 26). The trees have now been cut down, but that oval area has a cluster of self-seeded spruce trees in it which is visible on satellite images. Go to http://gridreferencefinder.com/ and you will find it at NX 52587076.

When the Forestry Commission were ploughing this area in 1977 in preparation for the planting of trees, three bodies were unearthed. Two were lying close together, only scraps of clothing surviving on their bodies but leather items remarkably well preserved. Buried separately was the body of a soldier, recognised by his long military boots. One of the two bodies buried together seemed to be smaller in stature than the other, probably just a teenage lad. He had a belt on his body, cut short to fit his smaller stature. Inlaid into the belt was a brass capsule that would have held the powder charge for a musket. The belt was most probably worn across the breast with the brass capsule facing downwards for easy dispensing of the gunpowder into the musket. Stewart McSkimming, a Scottish Power worker who happened to be working in the area at that time, removed the belt from the body and passed it to local historian and archaeologist Alastair Penman for conservation. It is in remarkably good condition and I borrowed it from Alastair for the conventicle we held (see Fig. 27). It is now in the possession of Dalbeattie Museum. There is a large nick in the belt, which has almost cut through it. It is likely that this was caused by the thrust of the sword that killed the lad, as Stewart is said to have reported that a wound appeared to have been inflicted upon the body below this cut. After the bodies were unearthed they were reburied and the ploughed ground around them flattened off. Then out of respect this area was left unplanted with trees.

I heard the rumour of the discovery of these bodies and for a time struggled to find out more details about exactly where they had been found. But in time I received the information that it had been near the Palfern Burn and the area around the bodies had been left unplanted. From my study of satellite images one particular place looked very promising to investigate, and when I reached it I found a prominent white granite cobble planted right in the centre of this area looking very much as though it was a marker stone (Fig. 26). I am sure I found the resting place for the bodies. We had a small granite stone prepared with the inscription 'Covenanter Martyrs' and this was dedicated at the conventicle we held there on 28th April 2013.

Almost certainly the three were killed in an encounter of some soldiers with a group of Covenanters, but we know nothing more. It could be that just two Covenanters were run to ground by a group of soldiers or they may have been two casualties from a clash with a larger group of covenanters. We assume the Covenanters must have acted in self-defence; but they must have been prepared to take up sword or musket in their defence if a soldier ended up dead in the moss beside them.

We don't know what happened there these many years ago. But the men very likely died in the Killing Times of 1684 and 1685. As mentioned earlier, in these years Covenanters were regularly run to ground in the hills and their bodies left to rot on the heather where they fell. No records were kept of such killings; the victims were simply regarded as 'missing', for none of their relatives or friends knew how or where they had died. For many years after the Killing Times shepherds would regularly come upon the bleached skeletons of Covenanters who had been killed in this way.

Maybe only the soldier here was afforded a proper burial at the time of his death. Perhaps the other two bodies were left lying on the moss until some time later a shepherd stumbled upon them lying there and laid them properly to rest. We will never know. But we honour the memory of them, these unknown men who died upholding the faith that was dear to them.

Fig. 28: Stone marking James Clement's grave by Kirkconnel Memorial.

14
BALMAGHIE CHURCHYARD

Sir Robert Grierson of Lag was one of the most feared persecutors of the Covenanters. In 1678 he was appointed Deputy Steward of Kirkcudbrightshire and the Earldom of Nithsdale. He was unrelenting in his search for non-conformists, hunting down and murdering a large number of Covenanters in the district.

On the 19th February 1685 he was travelling from Wigtownshire to the town of Dumfries escorted by two units of the King's soldiers – a troop of Claverhouse's Horse and another of Strachan's Dragoons, both under the command of Colonel Douglas of Morton. Lag had been collecting taxes and fines on behalf of his new master King James VII, the Roman Catholic brother of the late King Charles II. They stopped at the alehouse in Gatehouse of Fleet for refreshments. It was approaching sunset when the party was ready to remount and continue their journey. As they traversed Irelandton Moor a thick fog descended and that, coupled with the fact that they had imbibed ale rather too liberally at their last stop, caused them to lose their way on the moor. Lag was about to send one of the more sober dragoons back to Gatehouse to procure a guide when a light was spotted through the murk.

They had stumbled upon the farm of Gordoncairn. They enquired of the elderly farmer Gabriel Rain if they were on the right road for Dumfries. He replied that they were well off it. Lag ordered him to guide them back onto the correct path and, somewhat reluctantly, he agreed. After a while they came to Calfarran where the old man told them they would find a younger and much fitter guide. He took his leave of them and set out back to Gordoncairn through the fog.

Without ceremony Lag charged into the house of Thomas

Clinton, who was sitting at his hearthside surrounded by his family. Clinton was by inclination a Covenanter and had no love for the military and their bluster. Although not one of the more extremist of the Brethren and not being numbered amongst those who were outlawed or wanted for treason, he couldn't resist goading Lag for his practices. This only served to get Lag's back up and he began to question Clinton as to the movements and habits of his neighbours. He asked if he knew the farm of Mayfield and the man who farmed it, to which Clinton replied that he did, pointing out that it was a difficult place to get to. Lag decided that he would go there immediately, even though night had fallen, but Clinton refused to guide him blaming the inclement weather and the treacherous nature of the ground leading to the place. Lag then accused Clinton of being a Covenanter and told him that if he would not do as he was bade then there was a distinct possibility that he would entertain the troops by dancing on the end of a rope before the night was over. Clinton realised that he had pushed things too far, and to save his skin he needed to comply with Lag's request.

Ordered by Lag to lead them to Mayfield, Clinton set out at the head of the band of military, and led them the two miles across the treacherous moss to their goal, the home of David Halliday, a known Covenanter and wanted outlaw whose name appeared high on the persecutors' wanted list of rebels. On the way Clinton was persuaded by a Royalist officer to sing to them and he did so willingly with a lusty voice, some of the still merry soldiers joining him in the chorus. As Clinton had cleverly realised the noise which they made was so great that half the surrounding countryside would have heard them coming. And as the song which they sang was "Awa', Whigs, awa'" there could be little room for doubt as to who was abroad that night!

On arriving at Mayfield, not surprisingly the house was empty, the front door was open wide, a fire blazed in the hearth and a half-eaten and still warm meal was on the table. It was obvious that Halliday had fled – and not only him, for there was evidence that there had been others with him who had good reason to fear the approach of the Royalists and had fled with him. Lag was furious that his quarry had escaped and rounded on Clinton, blaming him for warning the rebels of the approach of the soldiers. It was pointed out by his soldiers however that it was them who had made him sing in the first place. An argument then ensued and one of the troopers was on the point of killing Clinton when Lag softened and agreed that he had been compelled to sing.

The soldiers made the most of the comfortable quarters which had been left for them and it was decided to delay the pursuit of the rebels until the morning. Clinton made himself useful by finding fodder for the horses and quarters for the troops until they trusted him enough not to bother watching him too closely. At the first opportunity he slipped away and his presence was not missed until it was too late.

The following morning the soldiers were up and saddled early and they set off in the direction of Dumfries in dispersed order. Lag instructed that everyone they met be stopped and questioned, all houses come across on their way searched and all possible hiding places checked out. He knew that the rebels he sought were in the vicinity as it would have been impossible for them to get far during the night. They hadn't gone far and were crossing Kirkconnel Moor when the fugitives, five in number, were spotted by some of the troops who found them attempting to hide in a rocky outcrop just over the hill from Lairdmannoch Loch. Knowing the uselessness of trying to outrun mounted troops, the Covenanters surrendered to Lag hoping for quarter but not asking any. They were found to be David Halliday from Mayfield, John Bell of Whiteside in the parish of Anwoth, Robert Lennox from Irelandton in Girthon, James Clement and Andrew McRobert. Both Bell and Halliday were wanted rebels with high prices on their heads.

By far the most important of the Covenanters was John Bell. He was the stepson of Lord Kenmure and a man of some substance in the area. He was socially Lag's equal if not, in fact, his superior and this fact was not lost on the Royalist who was a notorious snob. He and his kind had been pursuing Bell for several years without success. The Covenanter was the proprietor of Whiteside estate in Anwoth parish, and was a man of great prudence and religious scruple. He had been so disgusted at the behaviour of Charles II that he had joined the Rising that ended disastrously in the Battle of Bothwell Bridge. For the next six years he was a wanted fugitive. His home at Whiteside was taken possession of by Graham of Claverhouse and all his horses, furniture and moveables stolen. In 1681 Claverhouse again quartered his dragoons there until all of that year's fodder had been eaten up by his horses and the sheep eaten by the men. The crops were gifted to the local curate who accepted them with alacrity – a move he was to regret in due course when this greedy act marked him as a collaborator of the persecutors.

Bell had a number of lucky escapes before he was captured on Kirkconnel Moor. However that day his luck ran out. Knowing full well that Lag intended to kill them, Bell asked for a few minutes to make his peace with his God, but this was refused by the Persecutor even though Colonel Douglas tried to intercede on behalf of the condemned men. Lag swaggered over to John Bell and said to him, "What the Devil! Hae ye not had time enough for preparation since Bothwell!" He took a pistol from his saddle holster and pushed the muzzle right up against Bell's heart. Then he pulled the trigger and sped John Bell to his Maker. That was the signal for the killing of the others to begin, and as they knelt on the ground trying to pray they were massacred alongside him.

Lag forbade the burial of the corpses and they were ordered to be left on view to deter others from supporting the Covenanters. Eventually their friends were allowed to carry the bodies down to consecrated ground. Bell was buried in Anwoth churchyard, Halliday in Balmaghie; Lennox was buried in Girthon and McRobert in Twynholm. Their headstones can still be seen in those churchyards where they have been carefully and lovingly preserved over the last three hundred years. James Clement was a stranger to the area and he was buried where he fell. 'Old Mortality' provided a stone over his grave (Fig. 28).

On 11th September 1831 upwards of ten thousand people gathered on the slopes of Kirkconnel Moor to participate in an open air service conducted by Rev John Osborne in their memory. Soon after a monument was erected paid for by these worshippers (Fig. 29). It can be visited at grid reference NX 667598, at the NW corner of a small wood to the west of Kirkconnel farmhouse. Plaques on each face of the monument record the names of the martyrs, and also details of later conventicles held at the site. The main plaque has the following words:

> In testimony
> Of the feelings of the present generation
> On the 11th September, 1831
> about ten thousand persons assembled here,
> and after hearing an excellent sermon,
> preached by the
> Revd John Osborne
> From Psalm 74, verse 22nd
> Contributed a fund, for the erection
> of this monument
> To the memory of these martyrs.
> (Alexander Murray Esq. of Broughton
> having handsomely given the ground)
> Four of whom were carried to their respective
> burial places, but James Clement,
> being a stranger, was interred in this spot.

David Halliday's gravestone may be viewed in Balmaghie churchyard (Fig. 30) and reads:

Here Lyes David Halliday Portioner of Meifield Who Was

Fig. 29: Kirkconnel Memorial.

Fig. 30: Gravestone of the two David Hallidays in Balmaghie kirkyard.

Shot Upon 21 of Febr 1685 and of David Halliday Once in Glengape Who Was Likewise Shot Upon the 11 of July 1685 For Their Adherence to the Principles of Scotland's Reformations.
Beneath This Stone Two David Hallidays
Doc Ly Whose Souls Nou Sing Their Masters Praise
To Knou If Curious Passengers Desyre
For What By Whome And Hou They Did Expyre
They Did Oppose This Nation's Perjurey
Nor Could They Joyn With Lordly Prelacy
Indulging Favours From Christ's Enemies
Quench'd Not Their Zeal This Monument Then Cryes
These Were The Causes Not To Be Forgot
Why They By Lag So Wickedly Were Shot
One Name One Cause One Grave One Heaven Do Ty
Their Souls To That One God Eternally.

The stone makes clear that a second martyred David Halliday lies

Fig. 31: Stone marking George Short's grave, Balmaghie kirkyard.

buried in Balmaghie churchyard. On 11th July 1685, Lag and the Earl of Annandale were in command of a troop of dragoons in the parish of Twynholm. At night as they were riding back to their base they came upon two Covenanters, David Halliday and George Short. Realising they had no chance of escape, they gave themselves up. Annandale decided they should be taken prisoner and face trial the next day. However Lag ordered that the pair should be shot as they lay tied up on the ground. At first the soldiers refused, but when Lag threatened them with the consequences if he was forced to do the deed himself, they pulled their guns and fired.

The corpses were left where they fell, but were later taken to Balmaghie Kirkyard, where they lie in separate graves. As mentioned above, David Halliday is buried alongside his namesake who had already been martyred on 21st February 1685 at Kirkconnel Moor. George Short is buried in a separate grave in the churchyard (Fig. 31), over which a stone has been raised with the words:

HERE LYES GEORGE SHORT
WHO WAS PURSUED AND TAKEN
AND INSTANTLY SHOT TO DEATH
UNDER CLOUD OF NIGHT
IN THE PARISH OF TONGUELAND
BY GRIER OF LAG
MEMENTO MORI
AND THE EARLE OF ANNANDALE
BECAUSE OF HIS ADHERENCE
TO SCOTLANDS REFORMATION
COVENANTS NATIONAL AND
SOLEMN LEAGUE 1685

The church at Balmaghie is on a beautiful site, situated on a knoll from which one can look across Loch Ken to Crossmichael and the 17th century round tower of its parish church. Balmaghie church sits on an ancient site of Christian worship with early links to the priory of Iona. It may have been a monastic outpost of the Celtic church; and in the field alongside the church the Galloway hoard was discovered in 2014. But that is another story.

15
CROSSMICHAEL CHURCHYARD

Crossmichael churchyard, dominated by the church with its distinctive and unusual 17th century round tower, lies at the north end of the village.

Two Covenanters who were killed came from Crossmichael parish. James Graham was captured in October 1684 and, according to Kirkcudbright court records, came from Crofts in the parish. He was taken up to Edinburgh, where he was executed on 9th December 1684. From his martyr's testimony it is clear that he was a committed member of the Covenanting Societies. There is also a Covenanter named William Graham, most likely a brother of James, who is buried in Crossmichael churchyard. Mark Jardine in his online 'Jardine's Book of Martyrs' provides a helpful analysis of the historical records to shed light on his identity and what happened to him.

William's gravestone reads, 'Here lyes William Graham who making his escape from his mother's house was pursued taken and instantly shot dead by a party of Claverhouse troop for his adherence to Scotland's Reformation Covenants National and Solemn League 1682.' Jardine's investigations suggest it is much more likely that he in fact was killed in 1684. James' martyr's testimony makes clear that he had a mother and brothers. The evidence suggests that James Graham, and by implication William Graham, if they were brothers, had brothers who were fugitives and active in presbyterian dissent. These brothers lived close to Crofts in 1684, and most likely their mother did too. It would seem that the Graham family came from a dissenting family in Crossmichael parish suspected of harbouring fugitives.

The raid on the Graham family appears to have killed

William, a mere youth, as he attempted to escape from his mother's house, led to the capture and execution of James and forced brothers John, Robert and Thomas to comply with the authorities. So they died through a targeted raid rather than through random acts of violence. One account suggests that William was killed in March of that year. In this case James would have been run to ground and captured on a separate occasion in October.

16
BALMACLELLAN CHURCHYARD

Balmaclellan Church sits on a small knoll in the heart of Balmaclellan village surrounded by its old churchyard. It dominates the village; though up behind lies the grassy pudding basin shaped mound of the mediaeval castle motte looking down on the whole settlement. There is one Covenanter martyr buried in Balmaclellan churchyard. According to Morton in his book *Galloway and the Covenanters* many Covenanters had regularly taken refuge in a cave on Ingleston farm in Moniaive parish. However in April 1685, at the height of what was known as the Killing Times, the location of this refuge was betrayed to the authorities by Andrew Watson, a former Covenanter who had deserted the cause. Early in the morning of 16th April 1685, acting on Watson's information, Col James Douglas, brother of the Duke of Queensberry, along with Lieutenant John Livingston and a party of soldiers, stealthily came to the cave and captured five fugitives. These were John Gibson, the brother of the laird of Ingleston, James Bennoch from Glencairn, Robert Mitchell from Cumnock, and Robert Edgar and Robert Grierson from Balmaclellan. When the dragoons came up they fired into the cave, wounding one of the Covenanters, and then rushed in and seized the five. They were dragged out and ordered to be shot. Gibson's mother and sister, hearing of their capture, rushed up and pleaded for his life to be spared – but in vain. The soldiers however allowed him to speak to them, and Gibson asked them not to grieve for him. He was allowed to pray, which he did in a way that even impressed the soldiers. He read parts of Psalm 17 and John 16 and, after praying again, was shot dead. I quote here Psalm 17 in its entirety, for it is a moving psalm, and invite you to guess which verses he read out:

1 Hear, O LORD, my righteous plea; listen to my cry. Give ear to my prayer-- it does not rise from deceitful lips.

2 May my vindication come from you; may your eyes see what is right.

3 Though you probe my heart and examine me at night, though you test me, you will find nothing; I have resolved that my mouth will not sin.

4 As for the deeds of men-- by the word of your lips I have kept myself from the ways of the violent.

5 My steps have held to your paths; my feet have not slipped.

6 I call on you, O God, for you will answer me; give ear to me and hear my prayer.

7 Show the wonder of your great love, you who save by your right hand those who take refuge in you from their foes.

8 Keep me as the apple of your eye; hide me in the shadow of your wings

9 from the wicked who assail me, from my mortal enemies who surround me.

10 They close up their callous hearts, and their mouths speak with arrogance.

11 They have tracked me down, they now surround me, with eyes alert, to throw me to the ground.

12 They are like a lion hungry for prey, like a great lion crouching in cover.

13 Rise up, O LORD, confront them, bring them down; rescue me from the wickcd by your sword.

14 O LORD, by your hand save me from such men, from men of this world whose reward is in this life. You still the hunger of those you cherish; their sons have plenty, and they store up wealth for their children.

15 And I--in righteousness I will see your face; when I awake, I will be satisfied with seeing your likeness.

The other four were not allowed to pray and were

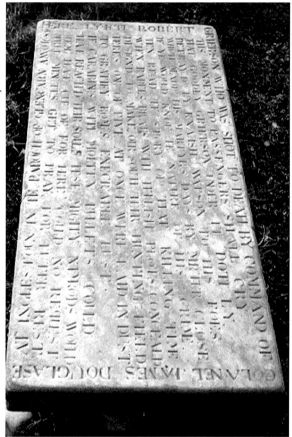

immediately shot. One of them was still alive and was thrust through with a sword, and as he died he cried, "Though every hair of my head were a man, I am willing to die all these deaths for Christ and his cause!" Gibson, Edgar, Bennoch and Mitchell were all buried in Glencairn churchyard, where stones were erected to their memory. A stone was also erected at Ingleston Mains where they were shot dead. It is located behind a stone dyke just before the farm steading at grid reference NX 797895. Grierson's body was carried back to Balmaclellan and buried there. His tabletop stone to the west of the church (Fig. 32) reads:

> Here lyeth Robert Grierson who was shot to death by the command of Colanell James Douglase at Ingles Toun in the paroch of Glencarn Anno 1685.'
> 'This monument to passengers shall cry
> That goodly Grierson under it doth ly
> Betray'd by knavish Watson to his foes
> Which made this martyrs days by murther close
> If ye would knou the nature of his crime
> Then read the story of that Killing Time
> When Babels brats with hellish plots conceal'd
> Designd to make our south their hunting field
> Here's one of five at once were laid to dust
> To gratify Rome's execrable lust
> If carabines with molten bullets coud
> Have reached their souls these mighty nimrods woud
> Them have cut of; for there could no request
> Three minutes get to pray for futer rest.

Rev Thomas Vernor, who had become minister of Balmaclellan in 1657, was ousted from his pulpit. By law, any person between the ages of sixteen and sixty who refused to attend the reintroduced Prayer Book services, at which roll-calls were taken, had to pay a fine, the money to be collected by soldiers billeted locally. Between 1663 and 1666 fines totalling £6430 (Scots) were imposed by the troops on 49 families in Balmaclellan parish.

Many of the confirmed Presbyterians escaped into the wilds, living rough, where they were secretly nurtured by sympathisers. Out in the wilds they would hold open-air services or conventicles, presided over by a displaced minister – and Thomas Vernor presided over many such gatherings. All the Glenkens ministers had been evicted from their parishes for being unwilling to accept the new Episcopalian system that the king sought to impose on them. Thomas Vernor, after being ejected from his position in 1662, had taken on the tenancy of a small farm on the shore of Lochinvar. His father-in-law was James Greir (or Grierson) of Milnmark so he must have sought refuge near to his wife's family. But he was always willing to meet his former people when he could do so safely, and they were always willing to meet with him. Many of the people were loath to have their children baptised by the curates and would wait for an opportunity to have them baptised by one of the outed ministers. It is on record that Thomas Vernor preached to a gathering at the Holy Linn on the nearby Garple Burn at which he baptised no less than 36 children at one time.

John Gordon Barbour in his 1827 book, *Tributes to Scottish Genius*, records the following tale. Around 1687 the persecution of the Covenanters relaxed somewhat and, although there was still some danger in meeting openly, the troops were less active in patrolling the countryside. And in the spring of 1688 Gordon of Grennan, who did not wish his infant son to be baptised by the curate of Dalry, requested of Thomas Vernor that he might perform that ceremony. The latter was asked to officiate at a general baptism of, not only Gordon's son, but other children who had remained unbaptised, and Vernor was asked to choose the location where this might take place. He fixed a day, and added, "I will take the top of some hill in the neighbourhood of Grennan and St John's Clachan." The choice surprised many people, who had rather assumed that he would have chosen a secluded place like the Holy Linn. There were several other infants in and around the village of Dalry that had not been baptised. Some of their parents had wished William Boyd, a young clergyman who had not yet been ordained, to officiate. He had been licensed to preach by the Cameronians. Boyd however declined as one not yet suitably qualified; but he was among the company that gathered for the baptisms.

And so on a morning of sunshine, after a very dark and cloudy dawn, twenty or thirty people assembled on the top of Mulloch Hill along with Thomas Vernor. From there the countryside of the Glenkens was spread out all around, in one of the finest views to be had locally. A prayer was pronounced and immediately after 17 children were presented for baptism and the ceremony performed with water brought from a nearby spring. Another prayer concluded the ceremony. Before the gathering broke up, Mr Boyd asked Vernor why he had chosen the top of a hill rather than the Garple glen. The venerable man looked up at the sun, then to some dark clouds vanishing to the south, and immediately said with firmness, "William, this was a very dark morning, but now you feel the sun shining in splendour. If I am not mistaken, the storm of persecution will soon blow over, and the sun of presbyterian prosperity fling his beams upon us. It is for this reason that I chose this elevated spot, where I can see at once the houses of Earlstoun, Kenmure, Ardoch and Barscobe, all of whom have participated in our troubles; and I hope we shall all, in a short period, assemble for divine ordinances with more freedom." "If that should take place," said Mr Boyd, "I wish you may be restored to Balmaclellan; and may I, under Heaven, be the minister of Dalry." "And perhaps," returned the veteran Vernor, "both of these may happen." After this the party dispersed, each going in peace to their own home.

And both of these things that Boyd wished for came about. In 1689 Vernor was restored to his pulpit in Balmaclellan. He continued there until his death in September 1716 at the grand old age of 85. At his death he was the 'Father of the Church', the longest serving minister in the whole of the Church of Scotland. You can see his flat tombstone lying on the ground a little to the north of Grierson's stone, which reads:

Here lies the corpse of Rev Thomas Vernor who served his generation according to the will of God in the gospel at Balmaclellan 59 years, died the 10th of September 1716 and of his age the 85th year. The last of the old Presbyterian ministers that survived the revolution.
Repaired in 1839. He shall be held in everlasting remembrance.

Interestingly, Thomas Vernor's younger brother Patrick was the oldest minister in the Church of Scotland when he died in 1722. Patrick was educated at the University of St Andrews and licensed a preacher of the gospel in Edinburgh not long after the Pentland Rising. Edinburgh ministers spoke highly of him to the dissenting ministers in London and it was there that he was ordained. These ministers recommended him to the East India Company and he was appointed chaplain of the ship President. However, while out in Indian waters, the ship was captured by the Dutch and the whole ship's company were taken prisoner. On being released, he arrived in 1673 at Britain's first Indian possession, at Fort St George, Madras on the Coromandel coast. The Company had been planning to send him up to the Bay of Bengal; however the chaplain of Fort St George took ill about this time and died, and Vernor (referred to as Warner) ended up taking his place until they could appoint a replacement. He was well received – celebrated as a very good preacher, and appreciated for his deep piety and gentle spirit. Vernor for his part was shocked at the drunkenness and immorality that pervaded life in the place and wrote to the Directors in London to alert them to the state of affairs. Those in Fort St George did all they could to persuade Patrick to stay permanently; but, concerned at the news of events back in Scotland, he decided it was time for him to return, and in August 1676 he took a boat home.

In 1677 Patrick returned to Scotland and preached at various conventicles in the fields, especially in Galloway, together with the celebrated John Welsh. Two years later, after the Battle of Bothwell Bridge, he was forced to retire to Holland. But he returned a short time later and renewed his field preaching throughout the western parts of Scotland. He subsequently suffered a long imprisonment and a variety of persecutions; though it is also recorded that during his imprisonment he was able to preach twice every Lord's Day to his fellow prisoners and a few others who managed to join them, so he clearly had an irrepressible spirit full of zeal for his Lord. On his release events compelled him to leave Scotland and he went first to

Fig. 33: Statue of Old Mortality and his pony on edge of Balmaclellan churchyard

Northumberland and then for a second time to Holland, where he remained until 1687. Taking advantage of King James' Indulgence, he returned to Scotland and was ordained parish minister of Irvine in March 1688. His father had purchased land at Irvine in 1656. The second husband of Patrick's daughter Mary was Rev Robert Wodrow, the well-known author of *The History and Sufferings of the Church of Scotland*. In his book Wodrow covers in great detail Vernor's cross-examination by the authorities after his arrest and imprisonment. It is also he who records that he was the oldest minister in the Church of Scotland when he died.

Shortly after the conventicle on Mulloch Hill Boyd went to Holland where he became friendly with William of Orange. He accompanied him to this country, and on his accession to the throne proclaimed him king at Glasgow Cross. He was admitted to the Church of Scotland in October 1690 and soon after ordained minister of Dalry. He is buried in Dalry kirkyard. The times of persecution came to an end and peace was able to descend once more on these hills and valleys.

Balmaclellan has another connection with the Covenanters. For many years the village was the base of Robert Paterson, the stonemason immortalised by Sir Walter Scott as 'Old Mortality'. He worked as an itinerant stonemason travelling around the churchyards of Galloway and beyond. No doubt there are many examples of his work in the churchyards of the Glenkens. But he made it his lifetime's vocation, alongside his more ordinary work, to erect, letter and renew tombstones to the memory of the Covenanting martyrs. Robert Paterson's wife came to Balmaclellan in 1768 and she supported her family by keeping a small free school there. Balmaclellan was Robert's base until his death at Caerlaverock in 1801 aged 86, whilst still working away at his trade and with dedication cleaning and caring for the stones of the martyrs. His wife is buried in Balmaclellan churchyard and Robert's name heads the inscription on that stone, which can be found to the south-east of the church.

Situated on the edge of Balmaclellan graveyard is a sculptured statue of Old Mortality and his pony (Fig. 33) which was produced by John Corrie of Lochfoot in 1840 and was for many years sited down the road at Holme House near the site of the cottage of Walter Paterson, Robert's son, who was also a stonemason. Tradition has it that before that it had been placed in Balmaclellan churchyard. It was moved to its present site in the year 2000. The statue is one of two Corrie was commissioned to produce for Balmaclellan. The other, of Old Mortality standing up, used to be outside the smithy in Balmaclellan and is now in Newton Stewart museum. Two other copies were also made by Corrie – one of which can be viewed at Dumfries museum, while the other now resides in Philadelphia in the USA.

Fig. 34: Barscobe Castle - the home of Robert McLellan.

17
THE HOLY LINN

You will find the Holy Linn, a waterfall on the Garple Burn, at grid reference NX 656808 (Fig. 34). It is best approached from the Dalry - Moniaive road, parking in a small roadside parking area at NX 653814. Across the road from this you will see a sign pointing to the Holy Linn, though there is not a clear track all the way to the waterfall.

During the time of the troubles many confirmed Presbyterians found places to hide in the surrounding countryside and sought help and sustenance from those who sympathised with the cause. Out in the wilds they would hold open air services, or conventicles, presided over by a displaced minister – Rev Thomas Vernor, the ousted minister of Balmaclellan presided over many such gatherings. Many of the people would attend these services rather than submit to the more formal and uninspiring services foisted upon them by the curates where the prayer book was read. Many parents were loath to have their children baptised by the curates and would wait for an opportunity to have them baptised by one of the ousted ministers. It is on record that Thomas Vernor preached to a gathering by the Garple Burn at which he baptised no less than 36 children at one time. The baptismal water was contained in the hollow basin of a rock, most likely down by the water's edge where the sound of the waterfall would have helped cover the sound of their voices. And thus this place became known as the Holy Linn. It may well be that baptisms were performed here on other occasions also. Near the end of the time of troubles Vernor is also recorded to have baptised 17 children on the top of the Mulloch, the prominent hill between the Holy Linn and Dalry.

It is a peaceful place. The Garple Burn winds its way

down in lively fashion through the trees. The soothing sound of the cascading waters of the Holy Linn fills your ears as you watch dappled sunlight flickering over the eddies and ripples of the stream. Amongst the old oak trees there are carpets of bluebells in the early summer.

What sustained these faithful people during their time of trial? I am sure the Word of God in the Bible was their greatest source of strength. It could feed and nourish their souls and give them a hope of a better day that would surely come, whether in this life or in the life to come. They felt that at times they were as aliens and strangers on earth, but they were longing for a better country, a heavenly one, into which in time they were sure they would enter in.

I am sure the Psalms were a particular source of strength to them, for David too had had to endure his time of exile, hiding in the wilderness and constantly trying to evade the attempts of King Saul and his soldiers to run him to ground. In Psalm 42 we see David caught up in inner turmoil, longing for the old days when he had led the procession to the house of God, struggling not to despair and lose heart in the loneliness of his predicament, at times overwhelmed by the cruel hand life had dealt him. We can imagine him standing alone in some wild place with the noise of a waterfall roaring all about him, and its waves and breakers seem as if they are overwhelming him and dragging him down. But in the midst of that loneliness he has an intense hunger to meet with God and find in him a way through his dark valley; and he imagines himself like a deer drawn in the heat of the desert to a quieter stream where it might drink deep and long of the thirst-quenching waters to revive its body. In such a way his soul thirsts for God, for the living God. And he finds in that longing a way upwards out of his despair to put his hope in God, in the firm conviction that he will yet praise him as his Saviour and his God.

The Covenanters found a freedom of worship away from the places of worship to which they had previously directed their

Fig. 35: Holy Linn on the Garple Burn.

feet. They discovered afresh what Stephen had declared before his martyr's death, that the Lord God 'does not dwell in houses built by men.' And they discovered also what their Lord himself had declared, 'that whoever drinks the water I will give him will never thirst' (John 4:14).That water would become in them a spring of water welling up to eternal life; and that 'a time is coming and has now come when the true worshippers will worship the Father in spirit and in truth.'

SOURCES

I drew extensively on two books in compiling the chapter on the historical context and would commend these two books to those who would like to study the history of these times in greater detail. These books are:

Scotland: The Story of a Nation by Magnus Magnusson. Published by Harper Collins in 2001.
Story of Galloway by John Robertson. Published by Lang Syne Publishers Ltd in 1985.

For the stories on the Covenanters of the Glenkens my main source was:

Traditions of the Covenanters, by Robert Simpson. First published in 1841.

At times I also found *Galloway and the Covenanters* by Alexander Morton, published 1914, helpful, and found much useful information in the Register of the Privy Council of Scotland, which can be accessed freely online through HathiTrust. I would also commend to readers Mark Jardine's online blog 'Jardine's Book of Martyrs', which is a wonderful resource for information on the Covenanters. A number of other books which I used as sources of information are referred to in the text.

APPENDIX 1

When I came to the parishes of the Glenkens in 1994 some folk spoke fondly of the conventicle that parish minister Rev David McKay had led at the Holy Linn on the Garple Burn on 4th August 1985 during which Mhairi Jardine of High Hardland farm had been baptised. In the year 2000 I decided to arrange another conventicle at the Holy Linn. It took place on Sunday 14th May at 3 pm. We held it in a clearing in the woods above the waterfall on the Balmaclellan side, having parked near Barscobe Castle and walked down from there. It was a glorious warm and sunny day with the bluebells at their best, and about 75 people gathered for that memorable service. After the service and a cup of tea I led the fittest down the steep slope to the river and a little upriver to view the Holy Linn itself.

It wasn't long after that that Bill Niven, the President of the Scottish Covenanters Memorial Association, appeared one Sunday at the service at Balmaclellan Church with his wife Florence. Soon after he arranged a meeting with me to discuss the suggestion that a sculpture that had kindly been offered to the SCMA by member Bill Dunigan might be sited in St John's Town of Dalry in recognition of the significant part Dalry played in the Covenanting story. I was supportive of that suggestion and a series of meetings with interested parties, including representatives of the local Council, took place in the manse at Dalry. They culminated in the dedication on 18th September 2004 of the Burning Bush sculpture, which had been erected just across the road from the manse.

But before that we had already held another conventicle at Earlstoun Castle to remember further stories linked to the times of persecution in the Glenkens at the time of the Covenanters. Below I list all the conventicles that were held during my time of ministry in the Glenkens, with grid references of the actual places we gathered. All the services on a Sunday were held at 3 o'clock in the afternoon.

177

Holy Linn Sunday (14th May 2000) NX 655807
Earlstoun Castle (Sunday 11th May 2003) NX 613839
Dedication of Burning Bush sculpture in Dalry (Saturday 18th September 2004).
NX 621808. About 250 people in attendance.

The Lorg and Whig's Hole (Sunday 12th June 2005) NX 667005
It was a day of torrential downpours as we drove north into the heart of the hills. But as we arrived there the sun came out and we were blessed with a moving service above the chattering burn.

Auchencloy (Sunday 11th June 2006) NX 603708
To get to the memorial there was a bit of a walk along forest rides after a long drive into the heart of the forested area. Perhaps the most challenging conventicle we ever held as the midges were biting like fury in the still conditions of that day. But we had to remind ourselves that that was nothing compared to what the Covenanters had to endure!

Blackwater (Sunday 17th June 2007) NX 618884
After a conventicle not far above the road we walked up the river, which is reminiscent of a Highland burn, to view the place I believe Dempster used as a hideout.

Holy Linn (Sunday 25th May 2008) NX 655807
Marscalloch (Sunday 14th June 2009) NX 603913
We held the conventicle in the front garden of Ian and Evelyn Watret's house.

Largmore (Sunday 30th May 2010) NX 574824
The conventicle took place by the road up the Garroch Glen, looking up the glen towards the house of Largmore.

Dalry churchyard (Sunday 26th June 2011) NX 618811

Appendix I

Conventicle highlighting Dalry's links with the Covenanters and preparing for the dedication of a stone to the memory of Alexander Gordon of Earlstoun.

Dalry churchyard (Sunday 27th November 2011) NX 618811
Service in Dalry Church prior to outdoor ceremony to dedicate stone in memory of Sir Alexander Gordon of Earlstoun.

Earlstoun Castle (Monday 11th June 2012) NX 613839
Conventicle partly arranged for visiting group from Presbytery of Debrecen in Hungary.

Palfern Burn (Sunday 28th April 2013) NX 526707
Conventicle held up in the hills to the west of Clatteringshaws Loch in Monigaff parish.

Halfmark, Carsphairn (Sunday 8th June 2014) NX 553929
Conventicle held just downstream from the ruin of Halfmark, where McRory is said to have lived.

Garple Burn (Sunday 31st May 2015) NX 643798
Conventicle held close to the ravine occupied by the Garple Burn where Covenanters used to hide, and looking up also to the summit of the Mulloch where a conventicle was held shortly before the end of the troubles.

Dalry church (Sunday 19th June 2016)
The conventicle planned for the churchyard was held in the church as it was such a wet day!

Upper Holm of Dalquhairn (Sunday 14th May 2017) NX 655992
Conventicle held beside the house where John Fraser lived.

Kells churchyard (Monday 12th March 2018) NX 632783

Conventicle arranged for the visit of the Moderator of the General Assembly, Right Rev Dr Derek Browning.

Earlstoun Castle (Monday 18th June 2018) NX 613839
Conventicle arranged for the visit of a group from the Presbytery of Debrecen.

Kirkconnel Memorial (Sunday 12th May 2019) NX 667598
Conventicle held at the memorial on Kirkconnel Moor in Ringford parish.

Balmaclellan churchyard (Sunday 3rd October 2021) NX 651791
Carsphairn churchyard (Sunday 8th May 2022) NX 562931

An audio recording was made of the 1985 conventicle at the Holy Linn. Andrew Blackley of the SCMA made a video recording of the service at Earlstoun in 2003, and produced DVDs of the services at the Lorg, at Auchencloy, at Blackwater, at Largmore, and at the Holy Linn in 2008. The conventicles in Balmaclellan and Carsphairn churchyards are available to watch on Youtube at 'Balmaclellan, Kells & Dalry linked with Carsphairn'. The channel can be accessed at: https://www.youtube.com/channel/UCAarMZusyIjo6F_Nk823STQ/videos .

APPENDIX 2

In places in the book I have given grid references to help readers find places to which I refer. A very helpful resource is provided by the website gridreferencefinder.com. If you type a grid reference into the grid reference box on that website you will be taken to a satellite image of the area concerned. This will help you get your bearings and see how best to approach a place.

In one instance (Dempster's hideout) I also refer to What3Words to enable more accurate location of the place in question. For the uninitiated, every 3 metre square of the world has been given a unique combination of three words. If you put in a grid reference on the gridreferencefinder website you will find that a combination of three words is generated for each individual point. If you put the three words given for Dempster's hideout into the What3Words box on the gridreferencefinder website it will give you a more accurate location point than the grid reference. Some readers who are more accomplished mobile phone users than I am may find this helpful!

INDEX